Reading "Nothing Wasted" is much like taking a long walk on a fall day with a friend who also just happens to be a wonderful story teller. Pastor Charles Reese will help you, as he has me, to remember God's goodness and faithfulness through both the terrific and trying times of life. The work of God in his and Enis' life has been bountiful as evidenced by the lives that have been touched through their ministry.

*After reading his amazing life story, I too am refreshed by the truths that "**with God** nothing is impossible" and "nothing is ever wasted!" I encourage you to take this walk, read these testimonies, and most of all to remember that in your own life there is a basketful of evidence that God has gone before you to make a way.*

> *Rev. Rick Collins*
> *District Superintendent*
> *GA District Assemblies of God*

I have been blessed to call Charles Reese a friend for many years. He is a man of honor and integrity. It is an honor and a privilege to share my perspective on his book, "Nothing Wasted." This book will help and encourage its readers in their everyday life. Charles has pastored and touched many souls for the Kingdom of God. This book will continue his life's work of helping others.

> *John Rayburn, Pastor*

Charles Reese has experienced faith in the Lord in a beautiful way and has touched many lives. I have been privileged to have made his acquaintance. I met Charles and Enis while serving in the Armed Forces in San Antonio, Texas. We met at a local church and with our kindred spirits, became friends right away. Our common interest was music as I played piano and he played the guitar.

Almost every weekend they would pick me up in their Volkswagen beetle and we would drive around viewing places of interest as they would sing in harmony. One song became especially real to me was, "If ye ever needed the Lord before, you sure do need Him now," especially with the way he drove. (No, I'm kidding.) The times spent with them made my last few months in the Service so blessed.

Charles and his wife came to see us in New York. One memorable experience was when his suitcase took a walk from the curb in front of my house as he went inside for a few minutes. He took it well and said that he believed that God would supply their need and He sure did.

As one who knows this author and the God he serves, I can recommend this book to you. It is a story of a man, his family and the faithfulness of God. You will be blessed.

Dominick Castanza

After life's storms pass and I look back, the most obvious thing I can see is the miraculous Hand of God that guided me through! This is how I feel when I think about these two heroes of mine. Charles and Enis Reese were sent by God to our house that hot summer day. There is no doubt in my mind this day was orchestrated by God Himself!

God changed the direction of my life that day. Because of the sacrifices this couple made during those years not only has God sealed an unbreakable relationship but I have the privilege of continuing Pastor Charles's ministry as senior Pastor of Covenant Life Sanctuary (formerly Barrow Worship Center) in Winder Ga.

I have never met a more selfless and giving man of God. I have seen him in action giving when he didn't have anything to give. And I have watched as the more he gave the more God gave him to give! God-onomics! He truly has a heart for people. I have heard him over the years as he would feel like he just wasn't making a difference saying " I just want to accomplish something great for God during my life".

At the end of the day, I don't know about all the others Charles and Ms. Enis have rescued, but I do know that I am one of those where God sent someone into a hopeless situation and gave life, life more abundantly! I dearly love you both!!!

Pastor Bobby Smith
Covenant Life Sanctuary

As the readers turn the pages of "Nothing Wasted", they will find experiences, miracles and just plain life stories penned by Rev Charles Reese. Charles is a true follower of Jesus Christ as evidenced in the pages of this book. My friend and fellow minster's desire is to inspire each one who reads "Nothing Wasted."

Rev. Jerry Abercrombie
US Maps Missionary

Nothing Wasted

Stories of God's Faithfulness

By Charles W Reese

Published by:

Spring Ridge Publishing
4626 Spring Ridge Drive
Flowery Branch, Georgia 30542
United States of America

ISBN: 978-1548431013
154843101X

Other Publications of Spring Ridge Publishing:

Quips, Quotes and Funnies, Vol. 1
Quips and Quotes, Vol. 2, Leadership
Quips and Quotes, Vol 3, Patriots, Politicians & Pundits
Growing Up Southern Style

To God Be The Glory

Dedicated to my Wife Enis

And our children:

Jodie, Shanna, Jonathan,

Sonya & Tonya

INTRODUCTION

A large crowd had gathered to hear Jesus teach about the Kingdom of God. Hearts and minds were opened to a Kingdom that was beyond what they saw in the natural. It was a Kingdom greater than they themselves. Lives were changed that day.

Recognizing their physical hunger, He asked the disciples what did they have to feed this mass of people. The answer was only a small boy's lunch. Jesus took less than enough and made it more than enough.

The small individual lunch of a child in the hands of the Master brought about one of the greatest miracles ever recorded.

Naturally we see the miracle in their eating the small supply of fish and loaves and as the Bible says, "They were all filled." He fed them the Word of God. Just as with the fish and loaves, with the Word of God He had an endless supply. And if that was not enough, Jesus gave instructions to His disciples to collect the fragments so nothing would be wasted.

And they did all eat, and were filled: and they took up of the fragments that remained twelve baskets full. (Matthew 14:20)

For me, life has been swift. The years have gone by so quickly and seemingly unnoticed. Age brings awareness that the events of my life were more than what I saw at the time. It is with the thought of nothing in my life being wasted that I want to endeavor to write this. It is an attempt to fill the baskets with the fragments, these testimonies, that I try to write these pages.

There are parts of our lives that are forgotten with the passing of time. Yet it was during those times that we prayed and asked God to work miracles for us with the promise that we would give Him the glory forever. So, let me say thank you for taking time from your busy schedule to read this.

My prayer is that somewhere in these writings and stories you will see the hand of God working in the life of this family, and realize that He loves you just as much and is there with you in whatever you are facing. There are stories of victories, stories of romance, and stories of disaster. Some of the stories are funny and some are sad and some show my humanity and my failures.

God has been with us through it all. This is about Jesus, our Provider, our Protector, and our closest Friend. These are stories that may be in your life, in the life of your pastor who needs a friend, but you will see there is nothing wasted.

Have you ever considered the thought, "nothing wasted?" Perhaps those twelve baskets were large bushel baskets that the disciples filled. Since there were twelve disciples, could it be that each of those disciples took a bushel basket full of fragments and went into the neighboring villages and began to share the food with those who would receive it? These people were not there when the miracle took place, but now they received the benefits of that miracle.

For instance, neither you nor I was there when Jesus died on the cross, or when they laid His dead lifeless body in a borrowed tomb, or when He rose from the grave, but for over two thousand years, we with millions of people have enjoyed partaking of that miracle.

His death brought life to mankind. His resurrection promises hope that we too can live again. Because of His mercy and grace, He has extended the gift of eternal life to us. I have accepted His gift because I do believe in Him. Indeed, He has changed my life.

Think about the times in your life when you were going through some tough times and you wondered why.

As you look back now, you see where God had control of the situation from the beginning. This remembrance increases your faith. Nothing is wasted.

The Word declares in Psalm 37:23

"The steps of a good man are ordered by the LORD: and He delights in his way."

He brings us this way because He knows where we are going. This probably is not the fastest way, or the way we would have chosen, but it is God's way. Could it be this is where the thought of "The Weary Pilgrim" came from? Yet the word for us is, "Be not weary in well doing."

The question comes to mind, "How can you call this doing well? Look at the situation! There is nothing *well* about it!"

Then the question comes, have you given your life to Him? Then trust Him with your life. Faith is the ability to give a positive answer to the question Jesus asks of you and me, "Do you trust me with this?"

God's miracles are like the pebble dropped into the still pool of water. The pebble, the dropping into the setting is wonderful but, that is not all there is to it. There are the ripples that are far reaching because they go on and on, and on.

We pray for the intervention of God into our circumstances, especially those that we feel are out of hand. We need His intervention, whether if by a flow of circumstances or by an out-right miracle.

But don't leave the table without collecting the fragments. Think about it. In your life experience, there is nothing wasted.

Just as the twelve baskets of leftovers fed many that were absent that day, the miracle was far reaching into distant villages and homes in need of a miracle. My prayer is that these testimonies will feed your spirit, lift your heart, increase your faith in His love for you, and strengthen your resolve to keep on keeping on.

Charles Reese

GOD HAD A PLAN

I enlisted in the Air Force on September 21, 1964 and immediately boarded a plane and flew to San Antonio, Texas. There I would spend eight weeks in Basic Training at Lackland Air Force Base.

I was given a week's furlough before reporting to Gunter Air Force Base in Montgomery, Alabama for Tech School. Like most other young men, I spent the week back home with my family.

Home was Newnan, Georgia, a small town about an hour southwest of Atlanta. I decided to check out some of the places I used to go and walked down to the pond where my friends and I had often gone swimming.

Not so untypical of middle Georgia in the late fall, it was hot this particular day.

No one was around so I undressed to my BVD's; ran out the large drainage pipe at the back of the pump house and dove into the water. I came up to the surface a long way from the shore.

As I began to swim back toward shore I noticed a stick protruding in the water as though someone had thrown it into the bank from a boat. As I began to move to my right, the stick moved. I realized it was not a stick, but a snake.

I swam in the opposite direction as fast as I could, got out of the pond and made my way along the shore to my clothes.

Then a sinking feeling came. I might have dived into an entire den of snakes! Do I have to say that this was the last time I went to that pond?

After Tech School, I came home to Newnan, again for a couple of weeks before Christmas. I borrowed my daddy's 1962 Studebaker pickup truck and trekked the two-hour drive to Murrayville, GA, to see my former Pastor who had taken a church there.

The Christmas party was at the "Club House." Enis Brady had a new 1964 Volkswagen and afterward some of the young people were going into Gainesville to get a hamburger. When we got to the bridge over Lake Lanier, the bridge surface had frozen and there had been an auto accident.

We turned around and drove north to Dahlonega. Enis said she needed some gasoline, so we stopped at a station. The ground was frozen and Enis slipped and fell. She was embarrassed, but we were concerned and glad that she had not been hurt.

She brought me back to the Pastor's house as it was getting late and it was beginning to rain lightly. I put my coat over our heads to keep dry as we were saying good night. I was tempted to try to kiss her, but decided against it.

The next morning as I walked into the church, Enis was standing in the choir wearing a beautiful white suit and a hat. *She* was beautiful. After church, I asked her if she had any plans.

She said no, so I invited her to go to Atlanta with me to get some pizza and she agreed. (I learned later that she was exhausted from the late night before and was planning on going home and getting some rest.)

This was before the interstate highway was finished in this part of the state. We drove down the busy two lane road.

A little puppy apparently had been hit by a car, but was still alive. You could see the fear in its eyes. I stopped the car and got the puppy out of the road. I had no ulterior motive, but it touched her heart.

When we got to Atlanta, the pizza place was closed. We ended up going to a counter drug store and had hot dogs. That was our first date.

Later she took me to her house to meet her mother. Her daddy had passed away recently. As we drove up the wide paved road, we came to a narrow, paved road, and then to a wide dirt road, and turning off onto a narrow dirt road I saw her house sitting at the foot of Wauka Mountain in north Hall County, not far from Murrayville.

The outside of the home needed repair. When I walked inside, the house had been completely remodeled. Enis explained that her Dad had died before he could get the outside completed.

On my second visit, she told me to not come back. It was too late. I was already hooked. On Christmas Day I had once again borrowed my daddy's Studebaker, bought two dozen roses and went to see her.

Her oldest brother and his family were there. I pulled up in the yard, walked up on the back porch and knocked on the door. I was not sure what kind of reception I would receive, but I thought I would just see.

She opened the door and with a big smile she received the roses. I was invited in and met the family. As time went on I met each of her brothers and sisters and their families. I was impressed with the love within the family and I fell in love with them as well.

As we dated for those few weeks I asked her many times, "Do you love me?"

Finally, she said, "If I decide I love you, I'll tell you. Until then, stop asking."

But every once in a while, it would slip out, "Do you love me?"

Later, back at the Air Force base barracks, the nearest phone was outside the building. Someone said I had a phone call.

Enis said, "I love you." It wasn't long after that I asked her to marry me. She said, "Yes."

Soon after, I had a three-day pass to leave the base. The weather was not bad, but they had predicted a winter ice storm. Regardless, I was going to see Enis.

I took my guitar and heavy amplifier. The only way I could get there was to catch a ride with someone and did so for "several miles."

It was cool when I left, but there was no rain. Before long it began to rain, followed by sleet, then snow. By the time I got to Atlanta, the winter storm had hit. The roads were iced and frozen. I called to see if she could come and get me. She said her mother would not allow her to get on the icy roads.

I reached as far as Clairmont Road in northeast Atlanta. I stood on the road in the freezing snow trying to catch a ride for the hour plus trip to the Gainesville area.

There were very few cars on the road and it was getting late. I began to realize people probably didn't have room for me and all of my equipment, so I took my guitar and amplifier and left them at a service station. I walked back up to the highway and caught a ride to Gainesville.

She met me at the old Colonial Store on Thompson Bridge Road in Gainesville. By this time, I had the flu and was so congested that I could hardly breathe.

Her mother said, "We don't let young men come to our house and stay, but under the circumstances you can stay in the back room."

The drinking glass was rattling as she stirred it with the spoon. "Now drink this all at one time. The last swallow will have the fire in it."

I was in no condition to argue. I drank it down, and WOW! She wasn't kidding. I thought, "This old woman has poisoned me!" But, the next morning I was as clear as a bell. All the congestion was gone.

"What was that she gave me," I asked. Enis said it was "horse liniment." The label on the bottle read, "Watkins Liniment, for external use on horses."

On one of my later visits, I asked her mother if I could marry her daughter. She said, "You don't want to marry Enis. She has a bad heart problem and when she comes home from work she is unable to do very much. I have to take care of her."

My mind was made up. She was the one I'd been waiting for.

I had always been a lonely person. Often I would pray for God to protect my future wife, even though I did not know who she was, or where she was, or what she looked like. I just believed God had the right one for me and that she was out there somewhere.

One day the Murrayville pastor was in Newnan and I ran into him at one of the stores. He said, "Charles I don't want you to come back. You are causing problems in the church. You have got all these girls after you and you have hurt them, and their parents are mad with me. Now, you are *not* going to hurt Enis."

I told him I had no intention of hurting Enis, but that I was going to marry her and I wanted him to perform the wedding.

On March 20, 1965, we were married in the little Murrayville Assembly of God. She was so lovely in the wedding gown she had made. It was a beautiful ceremony. My best man, Harold Lovern assured the pastor that he would make sure I would be there. He was concerned that I would get "cold feet."

My new brother-in-law, Ronald had a new 1965 Ford. I made arrangement to use his car to drive to his house and pick up *our* VW.

When we got out of the church, his car was gone. I thought he must have forgotten that I had asked to borrow it. So, we used the bridesmaid's car to leave the church.

When I pulled up to Ronald's house, the VW was there but his car was not. He came to the door and I asked where his car was. He said, "I loaned it to you!"

Wow! What a way to start a family tradition!

This was a time when a lot of cars were being stolen in the area. I got in the bridesmaid's car and Enis followed me in the VW to her house.

We later learned that some of our friends had pushed Ronald's car several miles down the road to attach tin cans to the rear bumper. They told us they were disappointed when they saw us pass in the other car.

We finally got Ronald's car home and began our honeymoon trip to Atlanta. We arrived at our friend's apartment around three o'clock in the morning. We were so thankful that we had gotten all the cars to their rightful homes.

AIR FORCE LIFE

I left my new bride with her mother and rode the train to San Antonio, Texas. I was now at my permanent duty station, Wilford Hall USAF Hospital on Lackland Air Force Base.

I ultimately found a small three room house on Quintana Road for our new home. It was located at the end of the run-way at Kelly Air Force Base.

Initially some friends helped to get the house ready. After that first trip to the house, my friends found other things to do.

One Saturday I was alone in the house painting the dining area. The Texas Air National Guard flew over the house and popped the afterburners making a thunderous noise. It sounded like a sonic boom. I found myself climbing out from under the dining room table.

Clearly, I was not aware of the weekend activity at this house so close to the runway.

This furnished house now with purple walls in the living room was ready for this new couple to move in and make it a home.

Finally, it was time to board a plane and fly to Atlanta. I knew she would be waiting for me.

I had determined that I was not going to run down the airport stairs to meet her. I was going to be, "Mr. Cool."

Then, I saw her.

It was like a scene out of a movie. She was waving and I was running to her waiting arms. The next few days we spent some time with her mother and then visited her brothers and sisters. We had no idea how long it would be before we would see them again. We were excited about the possibilities we would see as we began the next chapter in our lives together.

We loaded her things in her new 64 VW Beetle and drove the 1100 miles to San Antonio. She got a job as purchasing agent for one of the largest department stores in Texas, JOSKEY'S. She was a natural. Those over her department liked her and were very pleased with her work. Thus, our new life began.

Enis's mother had a very difficult time when her baby girl left home. It was quite an adjustment for her. She sold the old home place at the foot of Wauka Mountain, bought a mobile home and moved to her oldest daughter's farm. Letters came several times each week.

When Enis cooked, she would pour the bacon grease into a little sugar bowl that she kept on the stove. One particular surprise came after returning home from furlough to visit our families.

When we returned home, there were little black hairs on the side of the sugar dish. The lid was off and the grease was gone. We had no idea what had been going on.

One night soon after, she heard something in the kitchen. The kitchen was next to our bedroom and the door was open between the two rooms. Enis crawled to the foot of the bed, pulled the chain that turned on the light. She reached back and placed her hand over my mouth and pointed to the kitchen.

It was a SKUNK!

This one was very intelligent. There was a hole under the sink that was covered with a piece of bent tin. The tin had a brick on top of it to keep varmints out. The skunk would press down on the tin raising the brick up and then hurry around and go out the hole. They had a family under our house.

They were friendly until the Texas Air National Guard, "TANG," would fly over on the weekends.

Elizabeth, Enis's bridesmaid, wanted to come to our San Antonio home to visit with us. She was engaged to a young man in the army.

Enis's mother, Mama Brady, was a special lady. It was easy to love her and she treated me like one of her own.

Mama Brady was going to go home with us also. I had my Daddy's four door Studebaker Lark. We loaded up and made our way the 1100 miles.

We stopped and enjoyed the scenery along the way. Mama Brady had not seen an ocean before. She was like a child playing with her feet in the waves.

The young man came to San Antonio, found us and took his bride home. They were happily married for many years.

CRASH

I was a medic on ward B-9 at Wilford Hall USAF Hospital at Lackland Air Force Base. After serving a year on that ward, I was transferred to the Inhalation Therapy Department on the ninth floor. I often worked in the clinic that gave breathing treatments to the patients.

Many of my patients were children with Cystic Fibrosis. They would come in and refer to me as "Sergeant Greece," as they had a difficult time pronouncing my name, Sergeant Reese. I would fall in love with these little angels and one by one they would die. I had a hard time with that. One such little boy was named Jody. So when our first baby came I had determined to name *him* Jody. *Her* name is Jodie.

I worked swing shift often. That meant that usually I did not sleep in the first day and had to work all night. I usually came home very sleepy about the time Enis was getting up to go to work.

One morning, I kissed her, "Good morning" and said I was going to bed.

She said, "I don't feel good."

I responded, "Go back to bed. I am going to bed and get some sleep."

14

"I guess I'll go on to work."

I got up and kissed her good bye.

Then she said, "I *really* don't feel good."

"Then you can go back to bed, either way, I am going to bed" was my sleepy reply.

"I am going to go to work."

Again, I got up and kissed her good bye. I heard the door close as she went outside. I am drifting off to sleep when I heard the Volkswagen start up. The gears strip as she puts it in reverse. The sound of the engine was moving away as she was backing out of the drive. Then it happened.

"CRASH!"

I am telling myself to get up and see what has happened. She comes in the house with the sound of "Ooooooo," as she was shaking her fist up and down in frustration. I asked what happened and went outside to survey the damage.

She had backed into the utility pole at the edge of our driveway.

I asked, "What happened? Did the pole just come out to the middle of the drive and then move back over to the edge?"

"No," she said, "I was watching for you to pull the curtain back and wave bye to me."

She did not go to work that day, but went back to bed and I finally got some sleep.

I BECAME AN ATHIEST

It was during this time that I began attending the San Antonio Junior College taking *a* course, United States History. The idea was that since the Air Force was willing to pay for it, I should better myself as much as the opportunity was presented to me.

The teacher began the class by stating that the information in the books was not totally true There was no such thing as absolute truth.

"For instance," he said, "when you read the account of the Civil War written by an author from the South, you get a southern view point, and when you read the account of the Civil War written from an author from the North, you get a northern viewpoint. Therefore, there is no such thing as absolute truth."

However, I had given my heart to Jesus as an eleven year old boy and believed the Bible to be absolutely true. So I protested and stated that the Bible was true. Again, the professor said that if it were true then why was the four gospels that were written by four different men so different.

I could not answer the question. I began to question everything about God and my faith in Him failed this test.

I came home and told Enis that I was not going back to church anymore.

"So, don't ask me to go. I just don't believe in God anymore. I don't think God created man, I think man created God so he could deal with his weaknesses."

"Well, are you going to keep me from going to church," she asked.

"No, I'm not mad with anybody and I don't have a point to prove. It's just that for me I don't believe anymore and I am not going to go back to church."

Enis continued to attend church every time the doors opened. Each Sunday as she would leave for church I would get my guitar and play it while I sat on the sofa.

Something happened. It was as if God walked into my living room that Sunday night and confronted me with my desire to know the truth. When God speaks to us He speaks into our spirit man through our thoughts.

He said, "So you want to know the truth." The conversation began. (DO YOU KNOW WHAT I AM ABOUT TO SAY NEXT?) Of course, you do not. I make this point because I did not know what was coming next in what some would call "self talk."

He said, "So you want to know the truth. Well, that is honorable. Put your guitar up get a piece of paper and a pen and I will show you the truth."

I put the guitar in the case and placed it in its place, walked over to the dining room table, got a sheet of paper and a pen, and sat down.

"Would you agree that it is TRUE that there is life and there is death? Is that true or not?"

"Yes," I said, "That is true."

"Then draw a line across the middle of the page. On the top of the page write DEATH and on the bottom of the page write, LIFE."

"Now, would you agree that it is true that either I do exist or I do not exist?"

Again, I answered yes to that question. Note that with each step I did not know what was coming next.

"At the top of the page on the left side write, DO and on the right side write, NOT. Now, do you agree that it is true that either you do believe or you do not believe? Is that true?"

"Yes."

"Write at the bottom left side of the page, DO, and on the bottom right side of the page write, NOT. Now you were happy when you did believe, right?"

"Yeah."

"And now that you do not believe you feel miserable, right?"

"Well, I'm ok with this."

"Wait, now you were looking for truth and you must be truthful now. So, let's say you DO BELIEVE, and sure enough, I DO EXIST. Draw a line from the bottom left side of the paper where you DO believe to the top left side of the paper that says I DO EXIST. Well, you have been happy in this life and you are sure going to be happy over there."

"Now, let's say you DO NOT BELIEVE and you were right. I DO NOT EXIST. Draw the line from DO NOT BELIEVE to DO NOT EXIST. Who is going to be there to congratulate you on how smart you were? NOBODY! And, you have just missed the only opportunity you had to be happy."

"Now, let's say that you DO NOT BELIEVE and I DO EXIST. Again, draw the line from DO NOT BELIEVE to DO NOT EXIST. Do you know what that is?"

I stared at the sheet of paper in quiet contemplation for a few minutes. Then I heard Him say, "THAT IS HELL!"

I did not see any flashing lights; hear any sirens or angel choir singing. I did not feel His presence as I used to feel. This decision was not going to be based on feelings or special settings. This was based on my own choice to believe in Him, only.

This was probably one of the most significant choices I had ever made in my life.

Before this time, my relationship with God was supported by my Pastor, Rev. L G Gilstrap, his wife, Gloria, and my church family. They represented God to me. I saw God's love for me through *their* love for me.

Now, my relationship with God had nothing to do with church or church settings, music or any person. It was totally between me and God. In the years since then I have gone through some trying times, but my faith is in a loving Heavenly Father that has been so faithful to me.

Every experience I have had has proven that with God there is NOTHING WASTED.

THAT SPECIAL CHRISTMAS

Most Christmases we came home on furlough. However, one Christmas I was to be on duty. I was homesick and felt so bad.

I had gone to the PX on base and bought gifts for my family. Now, I would not be able to get the gifts to them. I remember standing at the window looking out across the road that ran beside our house to the two railroad tracks out in the field when a black 62 Studebaker passed by. It was like the car my Daddy had.

Seeing the car made it worse for me. In a few minutes, the car pulled into our drive. My family had driven the 1100 miles to be with us for Christmas. It was the best Christmas for me ever. My little brother and sister stayed with us for a while when Mama and Daddy went home.

By now we were expecting our first baby. The doctors were very concerned about Enis's heart. They kept a close check on her during the pregnancy. They decided they would admit her into the hospital two weeks before the baby was due and keep her for two weeks after the baby was born. The baby was two weeks late. That meant she was in the hospital for six weeks.

It was during that time that I lost quite a bit of weight as I didn't know how to cook.

I had gone to bed around 11:30 p.m. when the phone rang. It was Enis. She was upset and ready to come home because the other mothers came in, had their baby and went home. She was frustrated. Some were saying she did not know when she was in labor.

After midnight, the phone rang again. "Sergeant Reese, you had better get up here. Your wife has just gone into labor. I drove to the hospital and began the wait. The phone rang and they announced the baby girl was here. She was a beautiful baby. I wanted to name her Jodie because of the little boy that came to the clinic where I worked.

This beautiful little girl was named Jodie Marlena. After keeping her for two weeks with her Mother, I brought them both home from the hospital.

I would take Jodie with me where ever I could. I would pull her in the wagon even when I was cutting the grass with the push mower. She loved it.

For her first Christmas, we gave her a little red dog on wheels. She would pull it behind her as she was beginning to walk saying, "Augie, augie, augie" the little dog would turn its head left and right.

We had looked for a church in San Antonio like the one we had back home. There didn't seem to be one. We settled on Faith Assembly of God in South San Antonio. Brother Sam Mask was the pastor.

There was a young man in the army stationed at Fort Sam Houston in San Antonio who attended church with us. Dominick Castanza was from Queens, New York.

He told me of his father who was the first cook for Teen Challenge in New York. He was helping Pastor David Wilkerson reach the gangs of New York. Like his dad, Dominick was a great cook. We enjoyed many Italian dishes on the week-ends he came home with us. Today we keep in touch and are great friends.

There were those from back home who also found themselves in the service in San Antonio and found a warm welcome in our home. We were always glad to have them come and spend time with us.

COMING HOME

The time came for my enlistment to be up. This was during the Viet Nam war. I was offered $5,000.00 and another stripe to re-enlist. Enis was pregnant with our second child and the baby was due in October but my term was up on September 20. They offered me an extension for a short time until the baby was born.

We chose to come on home. I had a three-day pass and rented a U-Haul trailer. We loaded the trailer and had the freezer on the back so we could keep it plugged in. When I got off duty that next morning, with my little brother and sister, Alton and Judy, I began to drive to Newnan, Georgia.

Because the heavy freezer was on the back of the trailer I could not go very fast. My Daddy and one of his friends met us in Selma, Alabama. He drove the rest of the way home. We unloaded the trailer and I pulled it back to San Antonio to return it.

I still had some time before my enlistment ended on September 20th. We went to the commissary and loaded up on can goods, mostly beans. When my friends would invite us to eat with them, we were happy to accept. They would have great meals....and beans.

My Daddy was excited about us coming home. He had bought us a house and planned for me to manage a service station he now owned. I didn't want to disappoint them. After Enis and I discussed it we decided to move to Murrayville to be in church with my old Pastor.

She was anxious to move back home close to her Mother and the rest of her family, also. We chose to make Murrayville our home.

Our pastor at home had folks at the church looking for a house for us. The house was a mobile home with add-on bedrooms. It was perfect. It had everything that we did not have.

It fit like a glove and was only a few miles from the Church. Coincidentally, our new home was next door to the "Club House" where Enis and I had met at the Christmas party.

Our daughter Shanna was born October 25, 1968. I had taken Enis to her regular appointment with her doctor. After examining her, the doctor asked her how long she had been in labor. She said she was not in labor. The doctor said the baby will be here shortly.

She said, "I guess I need to go home and get my suitcase." The doctor said, you are not going anywhere except across the street to the hospital.

I took Jodie to the pastor's house and asked his wife to keep her and hurried back to the hospital.

When I got there, they congratulated me on having a second beautiful baby girl.

I had no idea what kind of work I wanted to do now that I was out of the Air Force. I knew I did not want to go into the medical field. A friend of Enis's who had distant connections with her family was in the insurance business. I asked if I could go to work with him one day just to see what he was doing and have a chance to see if that was what I wanted to do.

I met him that morning at the restaurant for breakfast. His supervisor was there and we were introduced. The next thing I knew, I am riding with his supervisor to the office in Athens, Georgia and taking a test.

There were questions like, "Do you like children, do you get angry" and others. I was to check on the right side or the left side. I checked each of them in the middle because, there are some children I like, and there are some that I don't like.

Mr. Grady Michael came back and said, "You've got to check on the right or on the left." I began working for the company the next day. I spent the first two years after my military service with that company.

My dream had always been to own a brick home on the lake somewhere, have a nice car and a secure job. We bought a three-bedroom, bath and a half in a subdivision called Wahoo Forrest. I could walk a short distance down the street to Lake Lanier.

We were excited as we moved to our new home, our first house. I remember walking over to straighten a picture hanging on the wall behind the new sofa. I said to Enis, "Well, I can say my life has been a success. I've done everything I've ever wanted to do."

The next few years were peaceful and good for us. I was driving my van to pick-up folks for Church on Sundays. My route brought me to Mama Brady's house. There were many Sundays we had dinner sitting at her table.

One particular Sunday was close to Mama Brady's birthday. Enis and I had invited her entire family to have dinner with us as we surprised her for her birthday. I drove past the road to her home.

She said, "Charles, you missed my road." I said, "Oh, I'll bring you back in a little bit. Just ride with me to carry these children home."

We pulled up into our drive and she was so surprised to see all of her children and grandchildren there. That was the beginning of the Brady Family reunions that continue on today.

WHO IS THIS JESUS FELLER ANYWAY?

One day I was selling insurance when I came to this old farmhouse sitting up in a field. The driveway had washed out ruts. There were children sitting on the top of the porch throwing things at the other kids as they raced around the house. It looked like something from a "Ma and Pa Kettle" movie.

As I got out of the car, they jumped down from the roof and ran to me. They covered me like fleas on a dog. I asked the lady about her insurance needs.

She said, "Mister, I am not interested in insurance now. It's all I can do to put food on the table for these kids.

After thanking her I returned to my car. I was so tempted to ask about letting me take these kids to church with me, but talked myself out of it. After all, it was ten miles over here, ten miles back and that was just to get them to Church, and then there was the return trip.

I drove down the country road a couple of miles before I stopped at another house. The lady bought an insurance policy. They had five children. I asked Mrs. Clark if she knew the lady that lived up the road.

She said yes, that was her sister. Mrs. Smith's husband had brought them from California and abandoned them.

I could resist no longer. "Mam, would you allow your children to go to Church with me Sunday if I came by and picked them up?'

"Do y'all want to go?" she asked the kids.

"Yes ma'am, could we please?"

With that I returned to the home of Mrs. Smith. She came to the door when she heard the commotion of the children once again running to meet me at my car. "I've already told you I don't want any insurance!"

"Yes Ma'am, but that's not what I want to talk to you about. Would you let the children go to church with me Sunday if I came by and picked them up?"

The kids began to beg, "Please Mama, please let us go."

"All the clothes they have are what they have on."

"They look fine to me. I'll be by around nine-fifteen.

With that five from the Clark home and the seven from the Smith home I continued my route that Sunday which included ten other kids I was already picking up.

When I got to the Church the first Sunday, we looked like a circus act. Those kids were hanging out of every window of my new 1968 two door Chevelle.

After this I bought a station wagon and later, a Dodge Van for the purpose of bringing people to Church.

One Sunday as we were on our way home, the oldest Smith boy asked the question. "Just who is this JESUS feller, anyway?" His tone was so emphatic it sounded disrespectful.

I pulled over on the side of the road, stopped the car and turned to him, "Just what do you mean by that," I asked. His response caught me by surprise. I was shocked.

"Well, I keep hear ya'll talk about Jesus, but I have never heard of Him before."

I took some time and explained that Jesus was God's Son. He was God coming as a baby and growing up as a man. He was without sin, but the people killed Him by nailing Him to a wooden cross. Because He was willing to die, His death paid for all the wrong we have ever done, or ever will do.

Later Bobby Smith said that week he went into his mother's bedroom, shut the door and got on his knees and prayed, "Jesus, if You are real, please come into my heart."

Today Bobby is the pastor of an Assemblies of God church in Winder, Georgia and his son is also ministering there. Through the years a good number of these kids, and some of their cousins, are serving the Lord as they have given their lives to Him.

LOSING IT ALL

Our community was plagued with a new strain of flu called "The Hong Kong Flu." It lasted for weeks. Because I was out with this sickness, I lost my job. I had gotten so far behind with the mortgage payments and we were about to lose the house.

Before this, I had made an agreement to purchase some thirty acres of land not far from where we lived. I had ordered the survey of the property and then the flu hit.

We had no money, no job, and no way to get any financial help. The bank was repossessing everything we owned on the next Friday.

That memorable Sunday evening we had gone to Church. The choir was singing. The Pastor was playing the piano. The Spirit of God was moving in that little building. At the end of the song, the Pastor leaned over the piano keys and began to weep.

In a few minutes he said, "We have a couple going through a hard time. The Lord has just told me we were to pray for them. I want Charles and Enis to come down here."

Enis began to make her way down from the choir where she had been singing. I was holding our baby, Shanna, and Jodie was sitting next to me.

I handed the baby to the person sitting on the other side of Jodie and made my way to stand beside Enis at the altar.

There was a message in tongues.

In a moment, the interpretation came, "I have seen your faithfulness. Your wife shall be as a vine and your children as grapes. I will meet your needs, give you the desires of your heart and I will make you happy says the Lord."

We made our way back to our seats. Enis took a card and wrote in short-hand those words. My thoughts were, "Meeting our needs is going to take a miracle, but giving us the desires of my heart? How could that be?"

One of the deacons was a manager of a Winn Dixie grocery store in the Atlanta area. He had given me a job there. I was making one hundred-fifty dollars a week. It was costing me fifty dollars a week in gas. My obligations required me to bring home over one hundred-fifty dollars a week. I was just not making it.

That next week was a week of miracles for us. I came home on Monday night and asked Enis where the card was that she had written those promises. She gave it to me.

She and I sat at the table and prayed. "God, You said You would meet our needs. I need a job in Gainesville, not Atlanta and I want to thank You for this new job.

At that moment, the Lord spoke into my spirit, "Put your coat on and I'll show you where to go."

"Get the kids," I said. "We are going to town."

"Where are you going?" Enis asked.

"I don't know, but I will know when I get there."

We drove to Gainesville and went up one street and down another. Around ten p.m., Enis said, "Drive down this street. I put my application in at this business on the right side of this street. I just want to drive by and claim this job in the name of Jesus."

We drove down the street slowly as we prayed. When I got a few blocks away, the Lord spoke again. "Turn around. You have just passed where you will be working."

I turned around, drove back up the street and pulled into the parking lot across the street from the business she was hoping for. The light was on and there was an old Cadillac in the parking lot. I knocked on the door. An older gentleman came to the door. Without opening the door, he asked, "What do you want?"

"I was just wondering if you needed any help."

"What do you have in your hand?"

It was a cold night in February. I had no jacket, but I had my hands in my pockets.

"Just a guitar pick," I said as I pulled it out of my pocket.

He opened the door and invited me in. He led me to the back office and opened his safe and pulled out his accounting books to show me the progress of his company. After about an hour I walked out to the car.

"Check back with me Friday," Mr. Heathman said.

As we were driving away, once again God spoke to me, "You've got that job." I knew in my spirit that it was a done deal.

Tuesday night after getting home I went to see the people I was planning on buying the land from. I explained my situation and said "I am sorry, but I am going to have to back out.

"How much did you spend for the survey," the daughter asked.

"Well, I haven't paid for it yet, but I will. The bill is three hundred and fifty dollars. "

"We will pay that. Don't worry about it."

That was the second miracle of the week.

Wednesday evening when I got home Enis was crying. "What's the matter?"

She slid a deposit slip across the table to me. It was seven hundred-seventy-five dollars and seventy-five cents. It was just enough to pay one month on each of our bills.

"Where did you get that?"

"Mr. Howard Parker knocked on the back door and handed me the envelope and said, 'Here, I know you need this. Pay it back when you can, and if you can't, don't worry about it.'"

That was miracle number three for the week.

Thursday evening, I came home, sat down and on a legal sheet of paper wrote down the bills and the payments due as well as how far behind we were. I folded the paper and put it in my coat pocket.

On, Friday evening I drove to the new job site on my way home. Mr. Heathman once again led me to the back office.

He said, "It was all I could do to not call you and tell you to come on to work, but I decided I would wait to see if you really wanted this job. How are you fixed financially?"

I pulled the paper from my coat pocket and gave it to him.

After looking it over a few minutes, he said, "You really are in a bind. We have a bonus system we pay after you have been here six months, but I am going to start you on it right away."

That was miracle five and six. Not only did I get the job, but had already gotten a raise and I hadn't even started work yet.

The following Sunday evening I stood to testify of God's awesome faithfulness in our lives. Once again, there was nothing wasted.

Enis got the call from the job she was hoping to get. They had decided to hire another person. She was devastated.

On top of the world now, with confidence I said, "Don't worry about it. It just means God has something better for you.:

Shortly after, she was offered a job at the Georgia Department of Transportation office in Gainesville. She would be making more money with great benefits and better working conditions. She loved that job and the people she worked with. She still talks about that job today.

GOD, IS THAT YOU?

Jerry Buffington was one of the radio DJ's on WGGA in Gainesville. His dad was a Baptist preacher in the area and their family went to different churches to sing as opportunity was provided. I had gotten word that he was looking for someone to sing with the family so I went to the radio station to see him.

His desk was covered with stacks of records and papers with announcements. I told him I played the guitar left handed and sang a little. The appointment was set and I was to meet them at his mother's house for practice. They were impressed and I got the position with the group.

Almost every week-end we would sing Friday and Saturday nights, and Sunday morning and night. It was a very busy time. Needless to say, it was not often I was able to go to our Church with my family. This schedule continued for a good while.

Later, our Church was having a revival and I was able to go every night. What a change in my routine! The preaching was good; the choir sang the glory down. There was a good crowd each night.

The preaching was convicting and people came forward and prayed for salvation, to be filled with the Holy Ghost and for any other personal needs they may have had.

I was in the altar each night, as well. I knew I needed God to do something for me. My attitude was less than perfect. In fact, it stunk!

"God," I prayed, "the preacher can't preach, the deacons can't 'deac', the ushers can't even do their jobs right. Now I know that if everybody else is out of step, the problem is not them, but it is probably me. Please help me! Do something for me, Lord."

I would hear a small voice interrupting my prayer with the words, "I want you to start preaching."

"Get out of here Satan! How dare you torment me like that! I am in the altar of a Spirit filled Church during a time when people are being saved, filled with the Holy Spirit and being delivered from your hold on their lives."

This went on every night until Thursday night. Again, I was in the altar praying the same prayer when the same little voice came to me.

Finally, I said, "God, is that You? If that is You, open a door somewhere. I don't want to join the ranks of the lay preachers in this church who are just lying around doing nothing."

I began to reason with God of my inabilities. He asked me what I could do. I began to list a few little things like, I could play the guitar, I could sing, I could teach Sunday school because I had had a little experience doing that.

I later found out that if you give God the little things you can do, He will increase your abilities to do more. It's like the little boy's lunch. It wasn't enough in itself, but when Jesus touched it, it became more than enough. There was nothing wasted.

I remembered that several years ago when my pastor was in Newnan we were coming from a baptismal service down at the creek where I was baptized. My Grandma was sitting in the back seat.

Just before we got out of the car he turned to my Grandma and said, "Sister Reese, I just feel God has his hand on Charles and will use him one day. I'm not saying he will be a preacher or not, but I just feel God will use him special."

After the revival service that night I shared with my pastor that I felt God had called me into the ministry. I could not believe how calm and cool he was at the news.

His response was, "I'm going to tell you like Brother Mayo told me, go start you a church somewhere."

As time went on, I began to pray and earnestly seek the Lord to find the place He would have me and my family start a new church. Looking back, I see that there was nothing wasted.

THIS IS THE PLACE

My Pastor, my wife, and I drove through several little towns with the question of, "Is this the place to start a new church?" We finally drove southeast of Gainesville to the small country town of Commerce. The railroad goes through the middle of this little cotton mill town.

As we were driving to the outskirts of town I saw a little boy walking down the sidewalk. It was late October. It was very cool but not bitter cold. He was wearing a coat, but had no shoes. It reminded me of another little boy from times past. I turned to my wife and said, "I believe this is the place." She said, "I do, too."

This was the beginning of something many will not understand, but I had just become PREGNANT with this Church.

My motivation was that I wanted the people of this community to know and feel the same spirit we had in our Church in Murrayville. Here was a little boy who apparently needed the benefits of that same spirit.

I don't know that I can adequately explain what I mean by that spirit, but I will try.

First it was a loving caring spirit. The people were genuinely concerned about you and wanted you to succeed.

It was as if they were aware of the dangers that would cause a young Christian to just give up and return to their sinful life styles, giving up on God and on the Church. When they asked how you were, it was not just conversation.

They were eagerly awaiting an answer with encouragement waiting to be given. It was the hug, the hand-shake, the pat on the back and the word that spoke life and renewed energy to a weary soul. Second, it was an action spirit.

I recall that in January of 1955 I was in the fifth grade in Newnan middle school. We lived just outside of the little run down mill village called McIntosh. Every Monday morning my school teacher, Mrs. Bartie Fleming would have scripture reading and prayer. Then she would ask for those who went to Sunday school to stand up.

"Now," she would say, "turn to those sitting down close to you and invite them to go to Sunday school with you next Sunday."

I was always one of those sitting down. I had no interest in going to church or Sunday school. My Grandma was a Christian lady and was always encouraging me to go to church with her. I went a few times, but felt the kids were making fun of me, so I didn't go often.

Late one Saturday night I was coming home from the movies. As I was walking the five miles down the dark path to my house, I began to think of those words, "You need to go to Sunday school tomorrow."

I made up my mind that I would try it one more time. The next morning, I went by my friends' house and asked them if they were going to Sunday school. They were getting ready and as we walked together, they informed me they were going to go to the new church. "Not me," I said, "I don't like them people. They took our school house and now we have to go to school in town."

We stopped at the corner of the street. To my left was the little two room school house I had attended. Straight ahead across Church Street, was the old established McIntosh Baptist Church.

After looking both ways I made my way across the street. My friends had turned left and were going to the new Church. Realizing they were not going to follow me as I thought, I turned and made my way to the new church.

The most beautiful young woman came to the porch and said, "Charles, won't you come in?"

"That's what I came for," was my reply. That was the beginning of a wonderful relationship with the "Spirit of the Church" that I was talking about. Her husband was the young pastor at the age of nineteen.

This young couple bought clothes for me several times as they saw the need. They would pick me up as they came by my house and take me to Church and bring me home. It was a few years later, in February they picked me up and when we got to the Church the Pastor said, "Charles, get in the front seat with Gloria. She has something for you." He got out and went into the Church to start the fire in the pot-bellied stove. She reached under the seat and pulled out a new pair of shoes.

When I saw the little boy with no shoes, I knew this was the place. Later, I found out his name was Charlie. Thank you, Father that there was nothing wasted.

PREGNANT WITH A DREAM

Pregnant may not be the appropriate word, but for me it best explains what I was feeling inside. There was an excitement because there was an expectation. It was in me, there was no doubt to that fact, but it was not in existence... yet. I knew there would be an Assembly of God Church in Commerce, Georgia because God had spoken it into my spirit.

I was working an insurance route at the time. I would find myself driving miles out of my way to go to that little town. I would argue with myself, "What are you doing this for? All you are going to do is drive through town, cross the railroad and drive back. You are just wasting your time." I suppose it made about as much sense as the pregnant mother craving dill pickles and ice cream.

As I would drive slowly through the town I would see people going in and out of the stores that lined the street. I would think, "That guy could be one of my board members one day, or that lady could be one of our Sunday school teachers."

I did not know anybody in the area, yet, I wanted everybody to know of the love of God that I knew. It had been demonstrated to me by the members of my home Church.

Our home church was in the community of Murrayville with a population of approximately one hundred. The Church choir was named, "The New Life Choir." With a powerful anointing and beautiful harmony, this choir was a major part of the music ministry of our church in this community.

It was not uncommon for our attendance to reach over three hundred at times. On Friday and Saturday nights the choir would travel to sing at different churches. Meanwhile, I was still singing with the Buffington Family.

One Saturday night they went to a church just outside of Commerce. Brother Harold Crocker, a lay minister in the community, approached my pastor and mentioned the ad we had put in the local paper. "I understand you are wanting to start a new church here in Commerce."

My pastor replied, "Yes, we have a young couple in our church that has a burden for Commerce."

"Have him to come and see me."

The Pastor gave me his address and his name. The next week I drove to his house, knocked on the door and introduced myself. He said he was glad to meet me, and asked me to come back to see him the next week. I was taken back in that he left me standing on the small porch and never invited me in to his home.

The next week, I again, drove to his house, knocked on the door and waited. He came out and said, "Let me introduce you to a fine Christian lady. We got into my car and drove down the street. He knocked on the door and went on in. I stayed on the porch. "JoAnn, this is that little preacher I was telling you about.

"This is Sister JoAnn Evans," Brother Crocker said as I came into the living room.

"Come on in," she said, "oh, Preacher, would you have prayer meetings at my house?"

"Yes ma'am. I would be honored to. Could you call and invite your friends and neighbors to come and join us?"

The prayer meetings began on Friday nights at seven. As we would sing our two little girls, Jodie and Shanna would sing the lead and Enis and I would sing the harmonies while I played the guitar. The prayer meeting continued until we rented a house on Jefferson Street the first Sunday in April, 1973. Once again, there was nothing wasted.

SMALL BEGINNINGS WITH A BIG GOD

The house we rented on Jefferson Street had six rooms and a hall way. It was an old house. The little windows that surrounded the front door had a few pieces of metal covering the holes where the glass once had been. The hall way was wide enough to have two chairs side by side on each side of the hall and leave enough room to walk down the aisle. Some of the young people from our Church in Murrayville came over and helped us patch holes in the walls and paint.

My dear friend and brother in the Lord, CW Fuller came over and built a small platform that came across the back of the hall and blocked the door going out to the back porch. We were given a small white pulpit. We bought a piano and an organ. I could stand on the platform and reach the keyboards of each of these at the same time.

We were given a strip of carpet for the aisle and a young friend that worked at a glass company in Gainesville cut and gave me the stained glass to go around the front door. Now I had a carpeted church with stained glass windows.

That first Sunday in April of 1973 we had our first services in the new facility. There were approximately fifteen people present.

We had a large plywood sign on the front porch giving the name of First Assembly of God. Services were held with the front door open. I would see people walking down the street peeping in the door to see what was going on.

There was a single mother that lived across the street with two children. She began coming to the church. One Sunday she did not come for Sunday school. I was concerned about her. After Sunday School, she and the children came across the street and she explained she was having some physical problems this morning.

"When I was getting ready," she said, "something happened to my back and when I bent over I could not straighten up without so much pain."

We anointed her with oil and prayed for her. "Are you feeling any better?" I asked.

"No. It still hurts so badly."

"Let's just wait on God." I said. We continued to pray and wait as she stood praying. In a little while I asked the same question. She said, "Something is wrong! I feel numbness going down my back."

I said, "Let's continue to wait." I was sure God was going to bring a healing.

She spoke again, "I feel a warm feeling going up my back. The pain is gone." At this she began to bend over and straighten up again and again. It was indeed our first MIRACLE!

That night I was ready to beat the devil up. Two people, beside my family, showed up for the service. There was no preaching that night. All I could do was cry in the altar. Indeed, the battle was on. But that young mother was healed that day and even though the day did not end like I thought it should have, still there was nothing wasted.

MAKING THE RIGHT CONNECTIONS

I had opened a bank account in the name of the Church at the local bank on the west side of Main Street. Every time I went into the bank, it was as if everyone behind the desks looked up from their work and watched me as if I were the enemy.

We had our first Youth Service and had two dollars and fifty cents in the offering. I went to the bank on the east side of the block. They were busy that day and I stood in line to open a Youth Account at First National Bank of Commerce.

While standing there, the vice president of the bank, Mr. Manley Gilmer came over and asked if he could help me. I explained I was the pastor of the new church, First Assembly of God at 105 Jefferson Street and had come to open a new account.

He said he would help me. "How much do you have to deposit in this account?" he asked.

I told him, two dollars and fifty cents. He smiled. He was very kind and cordial. He walked into his office after helping me open the new account.

As he got to the door, he turned and came to me and said, "Preacher, if there is anything I can do for you, please let me know. If you need to make a loan, I'll be glad to help you."

This began a long and lasting relationship with our new banker. It is always good to have a friend in the banking business. One day Mr. Gilmer asked me about our church.

"Just what is the Assemblies of God?"

"Have you ever heard of Jimmy Swaggart?"

"Yes, I listen to him every day. In fact, I take my lunch break at that time so I can get his program."

"He is one of us. He is Assembly of God."

"Oh, really! Well, that's good."

It was as if his perception of our Church changed dramatically, and now with only two dollars and fifty cents, I was accepted in the community.

When you are new in an area and people don't know anything about you, for some reason they assume the worse. I felt like many suspected we were a cult. But because we belonged to a great fellowship, the right connection was made.

When people are watching you to see if you are for real, if God is in control of your life, they look you over with a critical eye trying to find fault.

I later discovered there were a lot of Pentecostal churches in the area.

Then I wondered why God had sent me there. There was a group of people with common circumstances in their lives. They did not find an open welcome in the other congregations.

God knew what He was doing. I can state that there was nothing wasted.

THE MIRACLE WELL

We were looking for land to purchase so we could build the building. I found three and one third acres just outside of town going toward the interstate. My banker friend said he would lend me the money if the Georgia District would co-sign with us.

He also mentioned that he could sell me an entire block in town for the ten thousand five hundred dollars we were going to pay for this piece of property. It would be ten acres. I explained that I wanted to move outside of the town because that is where the future growth will be, I felt.

After we purchased the land I woke up one morning with the thought that I needed to check and see if there was water on the property as this was not always the case.

I went to the neighbors next door. They said, "Oh yeah we have plenty of water, unless we take a bath."

"What are you talking about?" My heart sank.

"Well, we went three hundred feet with our well and didn't get any water at first. Then one day we came out here and my wife dropped a pebble down the hole and after a few seconds, we heard it hit water.

However, the neighbor across the street at the KOA camp went five hundred feet and didn't get a drop of water. So, we are happy with the water we have."

In our Church at Murrayville, we had two brethren in the well business. They were brothers-in law. Brother Dillard Biddy came to bore a well for us. This would be a shallow well. It was a no water, no pay. He tried in two different locations on the property. Each time he hit hard granite.

I called for Mr. Murphy to come and look at the situation. He came and after looking it over gave me a gloomy report.

"Charles, I have been in this business for over thirty years and I am telling you now there is no water on this property. You are sitting on part of the Stone Mountain that runs underground through this area."

I called the City of Commerce and inquired what it would take to get water on the property. It was as if I had bought a piece of property that was not all it was supposed to be. It was going to cost two thousand dollars to have the city water line run on down to the front of our property and then extra to have it run upon the property and then there was the matter of a monthly water bill.

In my own simple way, I began to pray. "Lord, You are God. There is nothing impossible with You. Now this is Your property. It looks like You could put water on Your property."

Once again, I heard that little voice speaking to me. "Go down to the first hole, get a rock and I will show you where to put the well."

"Amen," I said, and walked down the side of the hill, got a large rock and began to place it where I felt God was telling me.

"No, move it over just a little. Your water is right there."

I called the District Office and spoke with, our District Superintendent Brother Aaron Wall. I explained our dilemma.

He said, "Charles, the Home Mission Board will pay to have the water ran down to your property, and that is what I would suggest. However, if you decide to go the other way, we will pay for that. But, if you go the other way and you don't get water, you will have to pay for the water to be run down to your property yourself. Do you understand?"

"Yes sir," With that I hung up. I knew what I had to do. If God could cause me to become pregnant with this Church, I knew He can put water on this property. He has said He would.

I called Mr. Murphy back. He came and I showed him where to put the well. "The bit has to be exactly where this stone is. Can you guarantee that?"

"Oh, yes, that will be no problem, but all I can guarantee you is a bill for six dollars a foot."

The drilling began the first of the week. Thursday evenings we had our mid-week service. I asked the people to pray that they would hit water within this next twenty feet. They had added another twenty-foot segment of drilling pipe on Wednesday evening.

Mr. Murphy said he would be there by eight o'clock the next morning. I got there at seven o'clock. I saw him running up the hill waving his hands as if he was being covered by a swarm of bees. As I pulled up on the property I caught him at the top of the hill.

"Did you get into some yellow jackets?"

"No, man! Look at that water!" It was shooting out of the top of his rig.

"I know, but that is water you have under pressure that you are forcing in, isn't it?"

"No! We turned that off thirty minutes ago."

"How much water do you think the well will produce?"

"Well over thirty-five gallons a minute."

"Is that enough?"

He said, "That's enough for a subdivision!"

To God be the glory for His faithfulness and goodness to us. When He speaks, there is nothing wasted.

We built the new building for thirty-five thousand dollars. That was a lot of money in those days. Our God Who can take less than enough and make it more than enough is still working, and there is nothing wasted.

ALL THINGS WORK TOGETHER

We needed a place to live now that we had given up the house at 105 Jefferson Street.

First Assembly of God in Albany, Georgia said they would purchase a used mobile home for us and have it delivered. We lived in that mobile home that sat at the back of the property up on the top of the hill. It was in this place that God would reveal Himself to me many times.

Later we were given a mobile chapel to use. This was a double wide trailer designed to be used as a church building. It had a bath room on each side of the foyer. The double doors led into the sanctuary. There was a platform at the back of the chapel and an altar rail. It came complete with nice pews.

We were excited to have this facility. There were a good number of new people that started coming to the Church.

We had been given a dog for the girls. Her name was Liz. She was a cockapoo. When she barked, it was as if she whispered. She had one eye missing. We felt we could give her a good home. Jodie and Shanna were so proud of their new puppy.

One Sunday night or early Monday morning Liz began to bark loudly. I didn't pay any attention to her. I was very tired and sleepy, and figured she was barking at some opossum or some animal.

It had rained that night. The next morning, I went to the Chapel at the bottom of the property next to the road. I noticed muddy footprints on the steps and the porch. I opened the door and saw that the foot prints led to the back of the Church to the platform.

I noticed my guitar and amplifier were missing along with the bass guitar and amp that belonged to a young man in the Church.

I thought someone was playing a joke on me. They have it stashed behind the piano, or under one of the pews in the choir area. I looked. Then I looked again. Someone had stolen this equipment. I couldn't say they had broken in, because we didn't lock the Chapel. After all, who in the world would steal from a Church, right?

They were gone! Now what to do? I didn't know what to do. I walked up behind the pulpit, looked out across that empty auditorium and a scripture rang in my spirit. *"All things work together for the good of those who love the Lord, those who are the called according to His purpose."* Romans 8:28.

I said, "God, I know You are going to get good out of this, but I'm telling You it is really going to be interesting to see just how You are going to do it."

There was a peace that came over my spirit. I just knew it was going to be alright.

I called the sheriff's office and reported the incident. They came, took statements and finger prints with no avail.

I went to a pawn shop and bought an old guitar that I could use. Ronny, our bass player was upset as well.

A couple of weeks later, on a Sunday morning the phone rang early. Enis got up from bed and went to the phone in the living room. I was right behind her. "Hello! Hello! HUH! Then she hung up.

"What? What?" I asked.

"Someone said your guitar is on the porch of the Church.

I got dressed and made my way down the hill to the mobile chapel. Sure enough, my guitar was on the porch leaning up on one of the rails.

This was no ordinary guitar. This was a Guitorgan. That is a guitar with the electronics of an organ in the body of the guitar. Each fret was divided into six parts. As you pressed the strings to the frets it was as if you were pressing the keys of an organ. It had the many organ settings.

This was a very expensive instrument, but there it was, setting right before my eyes. However, I did not get my amplifier back, but that was alright. I got my guitar back.

The next Saturday a young lady knocked at our front door. I recognized her as a daughter of one of our parishioners.

"My boyfriend wants to see you. He has something for you."

I walked out to the pick-up truck. There was the bass amplifier and the bass guitar. He explained that he has some young adults that hang out at his house where they do their drugs.

"When I heard on the radio about the break-in at your church I asked my kids about it. They said some of them had gotten high and came and took your stuff for drug money. The guy didn't want to give the bass back, but after about the third time of bouncing off the wall, he began to see his way clear. I apologize for what we have done."

The next Sunday night during the singing the front doors of the chapel opened and a group of young adults filled two pews. Of that group, when the altar call was given, a young couple came forward and gave their hearts to God. As I think back on that scene, indeed I can say with strong conviction, "Nothing wasted!"

GOD IS FAITHFUL

During this time, I was attending Emmanuel College in Franklin Springs, Georgia under the GI bill. The way this worked was while you are in school you get a government check every month. However, when you are out of school for the summer, there is no check.

Money has never been my motivation for serving any church or congregation. This was my baby. I felt the responsibility to make sure the bills were paid. In the beginning the offerings were very small and my wife and I took up the slack to make sure all the bills were paid.

Because I had no official training, I did not ask this new mission work to support its pastor financially. Looking back, I think I did them more harm than good. It was as if a bad attitude toward supporting the pastor was set and it was very difficult to change.

One evening the girls came home from school. As usual, they get a snack and get on with their homework.

"Daddy, what are we going to have for a snack?"

"Look in the refrigerator."

"We did, and there's nothing in there."

"Look in the closet and find something."

"We already have, and there's nothing in there either."

I stopped my preparations for the Sunday sermon, put the books up and told the girls that I would be back in a few minutes.

As I drove to the local grocery store, I quoted the scripture in Psalms 37:25, "I have been young, and now am old; yet have I not seen the righteous forsaken, nor his seed begging bread."

I knew I had no money in the bank, but I felt I had to trust God to catch me as I bought the mere necessities we needed and wrote the check. I am not encouraging anyone to do that, but God had the money in the bank before the check got there. I can testify of the faithfulness of God.

When I got home the girls had their snack and in a little while their Mother came home and fixed supper.

There was a time when one of my parishioners was in the hospital. The old car I had at the time got very low gas mileage. I knew I needed to go to see her, but didn't have the gas to make the trip. It was a hot summer day and I had walked to the mail box, picked up the mail and was sitting at the table. There were only bills and junk mail.

"Lord," I said, "I need some money today so I can go to the hospital and see Sister Carey."

The small voice of the Lord said, "Go back to the mail box."

"I'm not going back to the mail box!" I responded in my mind. Then I continued to pray, "Lord you've got to send me some money today if I am to go visit her."

"Go back to the mail box!"

"I'm not going back to the mail box! The neighbors will think I am crazy. I just came from the mail box and there is nothing there!"

"Go back to the mail box."

I made my way to the mail box, rolled my eyes, opened the door to the mail box … and… there was a white envelope. There was no name, nothing! I opened it up and found a ten-dollar bill. Indeed, God was faithful in spite of my stubbornness.

Once again, I saw God's faithfulness.

Don't get me wrong. I do not suggest you write bad checks, but I do suggest that you can trust the Lord in your hour of need. Oh, by the way, the check was good when time came.

I have shared the testimony about the money in the mail box as many times as I've had opportunity.

One day an elderly gentleman who was a local preacher and a professional painter came to me and said, "Do you know who gave you that envelope?"

"No," I said.

"I did. I was on my way past your road to the next town to paint a house. I had some workers waiting on me and I was running late. God spoke to me and said for me to go by and give that little preacher some money.

I said, 'I can't, Lord. Ten dollars is all I have to last me all week, and I have men waiting on me, and besides, I don't have time to get into a discussion with that young preacher.'

I drove right on by your road. The further I went, the sicker I became.

Finally, I said, 'alright, Lord.' I turned around and drove up to your mailbox. I could not find a pen; all I had was that one white envelope. I said as I put my last ten-dollar bill in that envelope, Lord I hope he gets it. I put it in the mailbox and drove away.

But when I got to the job site, a young man that had owed me for a long time said, 'Preacher, I need to pay you', and handed me a hundred-dollar bill. I had already written that debt off, but God is faithful."

Excuse me, but take a minute and look at the picture. There is a woman that is so sick. As she lies in the hospital room alone she begins to pray, "Oh God, please touch me. Send somebody to pray for me."

There is a young preacher who is praying, "Lord, you've got to send me some money today so I can go and pray for this sister."

And then there is the older preacher who recognizes the voice of his Lord when He says, "Go by there and give that little preacher some money."

And then there is the young man that God deals with and says, "Today you will pay the preacher that has given you the job of helping him paint."

Then there is the older preacher who in obedience gives all he has. And if that were not enough, God had said to me as I was on my way to the hospital, "I am going to come into that room and put My arms around her and she will be healed.

I came into her room and greeted her.

She said, "Pastor, I am so sick."

I said, "I believe God has sent me here today to pray for you."

As I began to pray, I stood by the window and the curtain began to move as if someone was brushing up against it. She sat up in bed, reached out and put her arms around herself as if hugging someone and said, "Lord, I just love you!"

Later I went back to the hospital to check on her. The room was empty and cleaned. The bed was made. I wondered if she had died. I asked at the desk what happened to the lady in that room.

"She checked herself out and went home."

I went to her house. Her daughter came to the door and said, "Momma came home from the hospital got dressed and went to work."

You see, God is faithful and there is nothing wasted.

TRUE MINISTRY

The young couple that came to the altar that Sunday night after the equipment theft began coming to Church on a regular basis. So did a few of the others in that group. He was a young man in his late twenties. He had a pony tail. In those days, that made a statement, but not a good one.

He needed a job and asked me to pray with him about finding a job. I asked him to meet me the next Monday morning and I would take them to help him find a job.

That morning as I was getting ready I began to ask God to send me some money that day without me having to ask for it. I drove to their house and picked them up and we drove to Gainesville and enquired in a few places.

He applied at a company called Cottrell's. He was a welder, and they hired him on the spot.

When he came out of the office I was standing outside. I glanced at the front tire on the car and realized I was in trouble. I had no money and the tire had no tread on it and an eye in the middle of it with the wires and threads showing. I didn't think we could make it home on that tire. What to do?

I went to a place in Gainesville called, "The Tire Barn." The young man came out and asked if he could help me. I asked to see the owner. The owner came out and met me.

I explained my situation and said, "I am a pastor of a new church in Commerce, Georgia and I brought this young couple to Gainesville to help him find a job. He has just been hired, but when I looked at my front tire, I realized I probably couldn't make it back home. I don't have any cash on me now, but if I could buy a used tire and have it put on the car, I will come back and pay you Friday."

He told his son, pull the car in and put a new set of tires on it.

"No sir," I exclaimed. "All I need is one used tire."

"Son, I have been in this business for a number of years and I know when a car needs new tires. Come into my office with me, please."

I walked into his office and sat down. He pulled out the large check book.

"Just the other day I was telling God that my business wasn't doing as good as I thought it should. God told me I was not giving enough away. What is the name of your church? I'm writing this check for one hundred dollars, making it out to the church, but it is for you. And by the way, I am giving the tires to you, too."

As I sat in that chair, the sun light began to beam through the window onto me. It was as if the Lord, Himself was smiling on me at that moment.

My new friend Bill Roper and I developed a lasting friendship. I would visit his business and we would sit in his office from time to time and talk about the goodness of the Lord. He was a man of faith, a man very close to God and God was using him to minister to other business men in and around Gainesville.

As we drove home that day, the young couple and I began to thank the Lord for His blessings on their new lives.

Even when we don't understand what is going on, God proves that nothing is wasted.

THE BUILDING BEGINS

New families were added to the Church on a regular basis. The spirit that was in my former church was evident here. People had a genuine love for each other. They cared if a person made it or not. There was community here. In time, we began to work on the new building.

At this time, my Dad began to help me with the building project. It was a good time. He and I got close as we worked together each day until evening.

When I finished one shift and started toward the parsonage, another member of the church would arrive and say, "Let's see if we can do some work, pastor."

I would go again. When that person had given out, and once again I started toward the parsonage, another person or two would come and begin their work shift. Many days I would begin working before 7 AM and would finish around 10 or 11 that evening. The building was beginning to take shape.

We were getting ready for the big day when we would have our first service in the new building. After all the earth grading, there was very little grass.

It began to rain, and rain, and rain. We were covered in mud. We had run out of money.

There was no money left to have a sidewalk up to the building. Our District Superintendent came by that Friday evening and saw the situation and donated the money to have the concrete side walk poured.

It was a great day. The rest of the world could see and reach out and touch the substance of what was once only a dream. The building was small. But, when designing the building, provision had been made for future growth.

A revival was scheduled. Announcements had been placed in the local paper and announced on the radio. Friday evening, I got a call from the evangelist. God was blessing them in such a way in the revival he was holding that he felt he should continue and would not be able to be with us. I felt like a step-child.

"What is this" I thought. "God, have you forgotten us?"

My wife and daughters had attended a ladies meeting in Athens. The guest speaker was a divorced lady named Tempe Brown. She must have been something. Every subject that came up in conversation with the family was interrupted by, "Tempe said."

I did not know this woman but already I did not like her. I had had "Tempe" up to my ears. I began to pray about who to call at the last minute to come and preach this revival.

Each one I called gave a good reason why they could not come. Each time I began to dial the phone, the Lord whispered, "Call Tempe."

Finally, in disgust I blurted out, "I'm not calling Tempe!"

After about the fourth try, I said, "I don't even have her number." Enis handed me the number.

I dialed hoping the line would be busy or there would be no answer. On the second ring, I heard,

"Hello,"

"Is this Tempe Brown?"

"Yes, it is."

"My name is Charles Reese and I pastor the First Assembly of God in Commerce, Georgia. You are not free this coming Sunday, are you?"

"Yes, in fact, I am."

"You wouldn't want to come and preach for us, would you?"

"Yes, I'd be honored," she said.

"Well, you are not free this next week to preach a revival for us, are you?"

"Yes, I'm free for the whole week. What time are your services."

I knew I was in for something, I did not know what, but it was going to be something. One night we got out of Church at eleven-forty-five. That was the earliest we got out the entire week. People were in the altars being saved, delivered, and I do mean really delivered.

There were many physical healings. The presence of the Holy Spirit was amazingly strong. Many were filled with the Holy Spirit. We saw great victories in the days following. Our Church was five years old.

I should have been on top of the world. But, it was about that time when some who had begun with us decided to leave. That was my first encounter with loss of people. I would lie awake at night and wonder what I had done to cause them to want to leave us. After all, I believed they really loved us, and that we were really close.

It was during those first five years that we gave birth to the Church. We saw people saved and their lives changed. Five young men in our ministry felt God's call on their lives. I thought that was what success looked like. But what does success in ministry really look like?

There began to be secret meetings with members of the congregation of which I was not aware.

I sensed in my spirit that something was wrong, but I could not figure out what.

Meanwhile, we had bought a used van for the Church. We were driving ten miles north to pick up some kids, and then ten miles south of the Church to pick up more kids.

It was Thursday evening, February second. The attendance was very low.

To me it seemed as if they didn't care anymore about the Church, or the ministries. I felt total rejection. The two kids from the town north of us did not come, so I had only the ones that lived south of town.

One of the members of the Church wanted to talk to me after service. My wife had gotten in the van to take the two kids home when I flagged her down and got in the van with her.

The two kids were delivered to their home and we started back to the parsonage. I was dying inside. I was so disgusted and discouraged. Our two daughters were sitting in the seat behind us.

I said, "God, just get me out of here. I don't care what it takes."

My precious understanding, encouraging wife reached over and took my hand and said, "Honey, we have just got to keep our eyes on the Lord."

"It's not me and God that has a problem! It's these stupid people!"

She moved her hand and placed it back on the steering wheel. The thought flooded my mind, "She is going through the same thing you are. Don't be insensitive to her."

I reached over to take her hand. She did not release the steering wheel to hold my hand. We began to go off the road to the right. She compensated too much and we went off the road on the left.

I feel I probably could have taken the wheel and corrected the situation, but I was in such a state of mind that I didn't even care. I turned to my daughters and said, "Just hold on, it is going to be rough, but we will be alright in just a little while."

The van went down into the ditch. Instantly I was flying through the trees. I was thrown through the windshield and into the woods. As I hit the ground I thought to myself, I don't care if I never get up.

Then I heard my wife calling me from a distance, "Charles, Charles, where are you? Are you alright?"

Then Jodie, my oldest daughter said, "Daddy, Daddy, help me."

"You had better quit feeling sorry for yourself and get up to check on your family. You have just had a wreck," I thought.

It took all the strength I could muster to get up. Then I saw my daughter lying on the ground with the front tire of the van sitting on her head. I cried out to God, "Oh God, I can take anything, but I can't take this!

Jodie and Shanna had come through the windshield behind me. Thankfully I came in front of my wife and popped the windshield out with my back. There was no broken glass. I flew through the trees. When I hit the ground, I felt no pain.

Then I saw Jodie get up and come toward me. She was not under the wheel of the van as I had seen. I had been hit in the eye with a limb while flying through the trees and now I was seeing double. With one eye, I saw her and with the other eye I saw the wheel.

Enis was still in the van. The door handle had jabbed her leg and she was unable to get out. The van had gone down the ditch and hit a large bolder. It flipped the van up on its nose with the back of the van hitting a tree and falling back to the ground straddling a fence.

I climbed the fence, stood in the road and flagged down the first car coming over the hill. The ambulances came and took us to the local hospital. Shanna had a broken back. She and my wife were put in a room together and Jodie and I were put in a room together.

The Church folks began to stream in with the question, "What happened."

I unleashed all of my anger and frustration on them. "Where were you? You caused this! I hope you are happy!"

Of course, I didn't mean it. I really didn't care at that moment if they were happy or not.

The next day, my wife's cousin, Jewell Gilstrap, a Pentecostal preacher, came and prayed for each of us.

When he left the room Shanna and Enis were in, Shanna said, "Mama, I believe God has healed my back." Then she began to sit up in the bed. She has never had any problems since.

All of this took a toll on me - I was burned out. A few months later, I resigned from the Church. Yet, as bad as this looked, there is nothing wasted.

WHAT NEXT

We were still living in the mobile home on the property. After the first Sunday not pastoring, the phone rang. It was a young pastor I had known for several years, Jerry Abercrombie. He was in the Church at Murrayville. He, too felt the call of God and had begun a church in Dahlonega, Georgia.

"Charles, where are you going to church this Sunday?"

"I don't know. I haven't given it much thought."

"Why don't you come and be with me?"

I began to think about Mama Brady. She lives in that area and she always has a good Sunday dinner. "I might," I said.

"No, I need to know."

"Well, if you see me there, then I'm there. But if you don't, then I am not there."

"No, I need to know. I want you to preach for me."

My heart sank for I believed I would never again stand behind another pulpit.

"Jerry," I said, "I'll never preach again. God did not call me to preach. I have just been fooling myself."

My friend was relentless. He would not take, "no" for an answer. So reluctantly I gave in.

I was dead spiritually. I had nothing left to give. As I began to preach I felt the touch of the Spirit of God reviving my soul. Those people began to respond. The more they responded the more my spiritual being came alive. When the service was over, I began to think, that maybe God had called me after all.

In the next few weeks I got a call to come and try out at the church in Bainbridge, Georgia. I told them I would pray about it. I really had no intention of going down there to pastor. I had not fully recovered from being dead. It was on another Sunday that I was asked once again to preach at my friend's church in Dahlonega. That night as we sat around their table he asked me what my decision was about the church in Bainbridge.

"I don't know. I guess I should call them and let them know something."

I got up and went into the den to use the phone and called the deacon and told him we would come.

BAINBRIDGE

Brother Gerald Jordan, our sectional Presbyter called me and said, "Charles, God is more concerned about the man of God than He is about the ministry."

His words spoke strength into my spirit because it assured me of God's love for me was not depending on my feeling of success or failure in the ministry.

We moved into town in a rented U-haul truck. I backed it up to the front porch, let down the ramp and began unloading. One of the men in our new Church came and began filling me in on one of the deacons and the deacon's wife.

I said, "I don't care about that just now. Grab this refrigerator and help me get it into the house."

Every ministry opportunity has its obstacles, and this was my welcoming committee.

The streets of Bainbridge, Georgia are beautiful. The old colonial homes hide behind the hundred-year old Oak and Cypress trees supporting the low hanging moss as they stand stately lining the streets. Down the street, the Flint River lies just over the hill that marks its territory at the edge of town.

Bainbridge is mostly a farming community. The men love to fish and hunt. The ladies of the Church are very much about the Bible studies and missions.

The town is small but self-sufficient. Everything is within three or four miles, including the shopping areas, the Church, the good eating places and the hospital.

When I arrived at the Church they were going to show me my office, but for some reason could not find the key. Finally, they found the key.

I opened the door and....

The roof had been leaking for some time. Pigeons loved this building. Because the building had not been adequately finished, they had found a way to roost on the outside walls of my office and pigeon droppings were streaming down the wall on the inside. Once again, I found myself having to work on the building.

That was alright because there was a wonderful attitude here. These people had a strong respect for the office of pastor in their Church. They banned together and we got the work done.

It was not long after we got to Bainbridge that Enis became pregnant with our third child. God had assured me a long time ago that I would have a son. I did not give up on that promise.

Our first child was born while I was in the Air Force in San Antonio, Texas. It was during this second pregnancy that she discovered she did not know when she was in labor. When Shanna was born, I had taken her to her regular appointment with her doctor.

After examining her, the doctor asked her how long she had been in labor. She said she was not in labor. The doctor said the baby will be here shortly. She said, "I guess I need to go home and get my suitcase." The doctor said, you are not going anywhere except across the street to the hospital.

It was such a short time from the time of becoming aware of the coming birth until the actual event. Now she is pregnant with our son.

We were going to do Lamaze so we had to go to a neighboring town thirty-five miles away because they were the closest hospital that made that program available.

One morning Enis told me she had dreamed that she was telling me it was time to go and I took my time talking to someone from the church. She emphasized that I should not treat her that way.

It was the morning of the doctor appointment. I had to go to the home of the church treasurer for church business. His wife was depressed. She had fallen and broken her leg.

In trying to encourage her I told her I had some good tapes she should listen to, and that I would bring them back by her house shortly.

When I got home I began gathering the tapes. Enis said, "It's time to go." The alarm went off in my mind. I asked, "Where is the suitcase?"

"Oh, we won't need that" she said. I got the suitcase and we went by the Treasurer's house and on to the appointment.

The doctor examined Enis and when she began to raise up on the table she realized something was wrong. The doctor took another look and realized the placenta had broken loose and was blocking the birth canal. The nurse got in the car with us and we drove to the hospital, a block away, and the doctor met us there.

He said that if this had happened anywhere else we would have lost the baby and probably would have lost both the mother and the baby. They presented us with our son Jonathan. Once again God was faithfully true to His promise. There was nothing wasted.

I preached on Sundays, had Bible studies on Wednesday evenings, and worked on the building every day during the week. The people were very supportive. We were loved, respected, and cared for by very sweet people.

Our Sunday school secretary, Sister Mildred Jenkins became a very close friend to each member of my family. She would come over and visit Enis and the baby. We ate many meals at her table.

Her husband, Brother Sam who worked for the city began coming to the Church on a regular basis. He gave his heart to the Lord and was a strong friend of this pastor.

Our initial contact there was Brother Scott Summerlin and his wife Debbie. They opened their home to us on our initial visit to the Church.

This was a loving young couple with one son at that time and later had their second son. He was there for us during the transition and proved to be a dear friend during our short time there.

One day he came by the office and asked me to go with him to meet some of the members that had dropped out of church during the time the church had no pastor. We went by this place of business, AAA Refrigeration. The owner was a big man, Mr. Orris Smith. My first impression of him was not favorable at all.

My thought was, "I don't care if you don't come back to the Church with that kind of attitude."

I was so wrong about him. Brother Smith became one of my dearest friends and our friendship has lasted down through the years.

He and Sister Ann had three sons, Matt, Lewis, and Greg. Greg was the youngest. He was learning to play the piano. We would go to their house and sing together as Greg played. Eventually he was asked to play for a local Gospel group.

Lewis worked with his Dad day in and day out. He was very good with repairing appliances and air conditioners. He didn't come to the Church, but he had great respect and love for his Dad.

Matt was Orris's first born. He was a big man. I saw him lift refrigerators to the back of a pick-up truck many times. His Dad did the same.

Matt later felt the call of God on his life to become a pastor. Many times, he would call me asking about a scripture or a thought.

This was a loving family and my family loved them.

We made the decision to get rid of our television. It was old and worn but we concluded we didn't need it. One day I came home and there in the corner of the living room sat a new TV. At first I thought I had gone into the wrong house. Then I realized what had happened.

Brother Smith who loved children did not want to see my children not have a TV, so he bought us a new one from his show room. There were also many times when they would treat the girls shopping in Tallahassee.

The Church was filled with such caring people. One such family was the Bill Alday family. Often Bill would bring us fresh vegetables out of his garden. His wife, Carolyn was a great cook. We were invited to their home many times. It was during those times that friendships were strengthened. I felt I could call on these people anytime.

After Church on Sunday evenings we had what they called an "Afterglow Service" at the home of one of the families.

Sister Moye was a faithful member and a wonderful Mother to her children. They had twins with nick names like Man and Lady. Cheryl and Lisa were the two older sisters. However, her husband, Carroll did not come to church at all. I was told that no one could approach him about religious things.

We had been there about a month when one Sunday evening we had the Afterglow Service at the Moye home. Everyone was having a good time. It became time for folks to go home.

I was standing in the yard with Brother Scott and Carroll. Brother Scott said good night and he and his family got into their car to leave. They had gone approximately one block and had stopped at the red light when another Brother began to talk bad about the family that had just left.

I said, "Hold that thought," and ran up the street and got Brother Scott's attention just as the light was changing. He opened his window and asked what was wrong. I said, just come on back down here a moment.

When he returned, I turned to this Brother, in front of Carroll and said, "Now what were you saying about this brother?"

The Brother stammered around and soon both men left.

Carroll turned to me and said, "Preacher, I like you. Have you got a little time to talk with me?" We drove around the town the better part of the night. A friendship was born that day.

One day I received a phone call from my Pastor in our home Church in North Georgia. He asked if I were sitting down and then said he believed God had spoken to him to have me come as his associate pastor.

I did not feel I had finished my task here, but then I questioned myself with, "How could I not give help to the man of God who had made such a difference in my life."

I talked with my wife and we agreed to go back home and work there in our home Church. After all, it was in this place that we felt the presence of God so many times; we loved the people and knew they loved us. It was in this place that I had felt the call of God to enter pastoral ministry.

We resigned among the tears and pain of leaving our friends. Milton Martin, Jr had washed out his cattle truck and he and some men from the Murrayville Church came to move us to Murrayville.

As we drove out of town we had gone about fifteen miles and I pulled into a church parking lot and my wife followed me in our car. We got out and embraced each other as we cried.

RETURN TO MURRAYVILLE

Our tenure at our home Church was short, about eighteen months. My experiences walking with God had changed me.

I was given the title of Assistant Pastor, but actually I was the youth pastor. It was my job to make sure everything at the gym was clean, the floors shined, the carpet vacuumed and the kids entertained.

We were getting ready for the Halloween festival the Church put on for the community each year. It was called the "Trail of Fears." Demonic oppression was in the air.

I talked with the pastor and told him I could not do this. I had seen too many "Christians" delivered from demonic possession or oppression, and it was ugly. I could not see that we would give the Devil his due.

He was mad. "You can fix hot dogs and serve food for all the people that will come."

That Sunday evening, I told the youth group that I would not be participating in the festivities, and why. One young man, a deacon's son, followed me across the parking lot. I heard him coming up behind me.

He said, "I could whip you all over this parking lot! But, doggone it, I believe you and I am not going to participate either."

He was the unofficial leader of the group. That year the "Trail of Fears" went back into the pit.

That ended the event at the Church.

The Church had rented a house for us a couple of miles from the Church. The owners supposedly wanted their house back and we had to move. The Pastor offered me what seemed to be a raise, but I would have to pay my own rent and utilities which meant that it was a cut in pay.

I shared with him that our arrangement was not working and that I would be moving on.

My Mother's family were from a little town called Homer. My Mom and Daddy lived there now. Daddy came to me and said a friend of his wanted to sell his land and I should come and buy it.

I was not interested at all. Daddy kept coming back and insisting. I made a ridiculous offer and thought that would end the conversation.

The offer was, "I don't have any money, I am not going to borrow any money, I am not going to pay any interest on any money. I might be able to come up with one hundred and twenty-five dollars a month."

Daddy said his friend said come and pick out what I wanted. His friend was willing to sell me the land at a very low price and finance it himself under those terms.

We had stored our furniture in a friend's basement until I could find a place for us to live. There were houses on Thompson Bridge Road for sale to be moved as they were going to widen the road. I bought one of those five room houses and had it moved to the land I had bought in Banks County.

The Pastor agreed to continue my salary for the summer as a severance pay. I worked on the house. We had at that point no water, no electricity, and no doors. I would work all day and sleep on the porch at night.

I was given a clear title on one acre on the back side of the property. I had the drive way cut in through the woods. It ended up being five tenths of a mile down the drive to the house.

Coming to our house was an adventure: especially when the rains began. Often, I would have to call my friend, Charles Denton to come and pull us out of the mud.

He has said many times when introducing me to some of his friends, "I've pulled this man through the mud many times" and laugh.

Living in the woods like we do, we see a lot of creatures. It is not uncommon to see two or three deer walking up the road.

One day Enis called me and said, "You are not going to believe what I am doing."

She then explained that while she was on the front steps a deer had come around our van that was parked in the yard and just stopped and looked at her. Jonathan told his mother to hold out her hand. She did and the deer came up to her and sniffed her hand. She was rubbing its ears as it was kneeling in her lap.

Then the puppies began chasing the deer and the deer turned and started chasing the puppies.

She was right. I did have a hard time believing it, but this was someone who would not lie to me. It had to be true. Then she showed me some pictures.

There are rabbits and squirrels. Sometimes you might see a snake. Most of them are harmless. We have had opossums also. But there is one visitor that does not sneak up on you. It is the skunk.

One summer night while Jonathan and I were away, Enis had the windows of the bedroom open and a fan was blowing the summer breeze into the room. All at once the fragrance began to change. It was a skunk.

Enis hesitated to close the windows because she did not want to disturb the creature. Finally, she felt she had no choice. She closed the windows.

The next morning, she got up and discovered the dogs had killed the skunk and brought it to the porch for her pleasure.

She woke up Sonya and Tonya and had them get a shovel and put the lifeless skunk in a black plastic bag. She then tied the bag to the outside mirror of the Church van and drove off to find a place to dispose of it.

When she got to the place she had planned to throw the skunk, she could not get the bag untied from the mirror. She came home and got a small saw to cut the bag from the mirror. Then she and the girls drove down the road and was about to do the unpardonable and throw the garbage bag down the hill on the side of the road.

As she was approaching the site, a car pulled up behind her. She drove on to the end of the road and turned around. Making sure the coast was clear, she drove back to the spot and, you guessed it! A car pulled up behind her. She continued to drive past the spot again and find a place to turn around.

This time she came to the "drop zone." She stopped and tossed the bag with its stinking contents.

A car pulled up beside her and an angry man said, "You go back and get it! I live in this community and I am tired of people throwing their trash out on the side of the road here. You go back and get it!"

He was irate. She tried to explain that it was a skunk. "I don't care what it is. Go back and get it!"

It looked as if he was writing down the tag number. Of course, that was unnecessary since the name of the Church was on the side of the van.

Because my wife is a law-abiding citizen and a good Christian, she got out of the van and began trying to climb down the embankment to retrieve the bag. However, the briars and thorns prevented the retrieval. So, understanding that her sins had found her out, she did the only thing she could think of. She went to the Sheriff's department and turned herself in.

They just had a good laugh and then expressed that their concern was with the gentleman who had spoken to her demanding that she retrieve the bag.

We came back to pastor the First Assembly of God in Commerce for the second time. This time we served for eight years. Again, there was no salary. I worked secular jobs and paid most of the bills for the Church out of my pocket. I could not have done that if God had not provided.

For some time, I worked as a used car salesman at Milton Martin Toyota in Gainesville. This kind of selling was different. I had to learn how to keep a positive attitude even when my sales were down. I went through a time when I felt I could not give a car away.

One day the sales manager came to work on his day off. I had tried to talk to several customers without any success. He asked me to go for a ride with him. We drove out to some property he was trying to buy.

He said, "We have been watching you, Charles. We have seen salesmen come and go. Some have it and some don't. You just need to keep to your preaching. You don't have it."

"Well, how long do I have? Do I walk home from here? Do I go back to the car lot? Just what do you want me to do?"

He said, "How long do you need to work out a notice?"

"Well, I need to the end of the month if that would be possible."

"Ok, you have to the end of the month. But I would suggest you look for something else to do."

We drove back to the car lot. I got in the demo car and drove home. I had a good long talk with myself. All my life I have been told I couldn't do certain things. As I thought about that list, I realized that I had achieved the things they said I would not be able to do.

The next morning, I came into the office and asked to see the two managers. They were expecting me to resign.

I said, "I appreciate your opinions. I know you have been in this business for many years and have a lot of experience. However, there is another opinion that really matters and that's my opinion. If you can sell a car, I can sell a car."

"How many cars do you want me to put down for you?" the manager asked.

We would write the number of cars we expected to sell each month on a board. I said, "Put me down for 15 cars." They grinned as the manager wrote the number on the board. That month I sold 21 cars.

Later I bought half interest in my own car lot on the Atlanta Highway in Gainesville.

My partner worked hard for a while then he just sat all day while I did the work. When he asked me to buy him out, of course I couldn't because I had sunk all I had to start the business with him. Then he said he should buy me out at a loss. I was not interested in doing that either. Then I began to realize that if I didn't take his offer, I would end up with nothing.

I guess I got what I deserved. God said to not be unequally yoked yet I ignored this truth and went into a partnership with a non-believer.

LOSING MY BEST FRIEND

My dad was having a rough time physically. He was always a heavy smoker. Mama encouraged him to go to the doctor. He would take a lot of cough syrup to help with the coughing. Now he was coughing up blood. The doctor put him in the hospital. Jodie and I went to see him. We sat for a long time talking.

As we started to leave, I got to the door and he called me back. "Charles."

"Yes sir."

"Who was that with you?"

"That is Jodie, Daddy, my oldest daughter. Don't you remember her?"

"That's what I thought."

I knew at that point his brain was not getting enough oxygen and now he was beginning to not know things.

The next day I met the doctor in the hall as he was coming out of Daddy's room. "What do you think, Doc?"

"Your Daddy is eaten up with cancer. He may have three weeks to live."

"Thank you."

The doctor walked on down the hall and I went into Daddy's room.

"Do you know what the doctor said, Daddy?"

"No."

"He said you were eaten up with cancer and you didn't have long to live."

"I don't doubt it" he said.

"Are you up to going to Newnan?"

"I'm up to going to Newnan if going to Newnan is up to me."

Then I told him I would be back in a little while and we would go. I went home and called my uncle William and told him I was bringing Daddy home to die and would he see if he could get some furniture in the old house.

Enis and I went to the hospital and checked Daddy out and began the trip to Newnan. He would groan with every little bump in the road. When we got to the old home place we got him into bed. Some of his old friends came by to see him. They would laugh and talk about old times and things. He seemed to gain a new strength.

In a couple of weeks, he was admitted to the hospital in Newnan. I sat up with him every night. We would talk as we grew closer than ever. His main concern was who was going to take care of my sister's two girls that were living with him and Mama. I assured him I would see that they were taken care of.

He had given his heart to the Lord a few years ago and always wanted to be baptized. I made arrangements with a local Baptist Church to use their facilities to baptize him.

He had an old friend he had worked with who had died years earlier and his widow asked to stay with him that Saturday night.

When I came into the room the next morning he said, "Charles, don't blame her. It was my fault."

"What are you talking about, Daddy?"

"I was dreaming we were having a party and someone knocked on the door. I got up to answer the door and I tripped over the IV pole and they said it broke my hip."

I was so sorry to hear that because that meant the he would not be baptized as we had planned.

The doctor said there was no use in trying to set his leg. He would not live long enough for it to heal, and now the cancer was in his bones.

THE DREAM

I was in such grief. One night I had a dream that seemed more than just a dream. It was real.

I was walking down the street in Newnan. Someone was with me, but there was no "BODY" with me.

This person said, "This is the place" and he stood on the side walk as I walked up the walk to go up the steps.

A man dressed in a dark suit opened the door and said, "Come in. You are at the right place."

He led me into the hallway and then into a large room on the right. People were sitting on a long sofa.

He said, "Have a seat; it will be just a moment." I stood looking around with my arms folded.

Then I thought, "He said have a seat" so I sat down on the sofa. People were talking low. I was not trying to understand what they were saying, but I noticed that while they talked, they did not move their mouths.

In a few minutes, Daddy came in the door across the room in front of me. He was wearing the suit we had buried him in.

I got up and went to him. I put my arms around him and began to hug him. Then it came to me that he was supposed to be dead.

I said, "Daddy, you are supposed to be dead. What are you doing here?"

"I know I'm dead," he said, "you don't have to remind me. They were kind enough to let me come and see you one more time. You know I told you that when I died ya'll were not supposed to be crying, but were to have a party. I have not heard the partying, but I am hearing you cry. You are bothering me. You've got to go on with your life, son. It is so beautiful here. I'll see you in a few days," as he patted me on my back.

With that I released my embrace and he walked out the door. It was as if he disappeared there. Instantly I woke up. I knew this was real. Ok, it was real for me.

SONYA AND TONYA

After my Daddy's death, my sister left her two daughters with Mama and ran away with a man who left his wife and family for her. The girls were placed in a foster home.

When we heard they were going to be placed in separate foster homes, we knew we had to do something for these girls. There was no one else in the family that could or would help.

Enis gave up her job to stay home with these two girls and our son who was about the same age. It was a time when I could not find work. We were behind with all of our bills. Enis was amazing in putting together meals when it seemed we had nothing for her to cook. Somehow, she managed to perform the miracle.

It was my birthday. I had been out looking for work all day without any success. Enis had promised the children they would go on a picnic. She had made some home-made soup for the occasion.

When I got home, Jonathan had wrapped a knife that I had given him some time back, and presented it to me for my birthday gift from him. I felt like a total failure.

Enis wrote in those days, "I busied myself during the day so I would not have to think about our circumstances. At night, I couldn't sleep and would often find myself walking up and down the road praying. One night we had a visitor in our bedroom. He was dressed in white and he stood at the foot of our bed.

He said, 'I have just come to sit with you while you sleep.' I slept the best that night. I have wondered since then why he did not say anything about helping us with our situation."

It was during this time when I was selling T-shirts to Emmanuel College.

Brian James was in charge of the campus café. Shanna had signed up for classes at Emanuel. One day she rode with me to meet Brian on one of my business deals. He was in his family's yard picking up pecans.

We got out of the car and I introduced them. During the days that followed I asked her if she ever saw him. She said she has seen him but she thought he had not seen her.

My thought was that he could not be that blind. She was (and still is) a beautiful girl. One day she called me and said he had asked her for a date. A few weeks later she called and said, "Daddy, I have found the man of your dreams."

"Hold it," I said, "I haven't been dreaming about a man."

"Oh, I meant for me. He has asked me to marry him."

I was very happy for her. I questioned her to make sure she was in love with him, and not just the setting. She felt I was against her marrying him, but that was not true. I just wanted her to be sure of her decision. We loved Brian as much as we loved our own children.

The day came when Shanna went to the hospital in labor. Evan Luke James was born that evening.

We were so happy for them. Brian's Mother and Dad had moved to Oklahoma to serve in the General Council office of the Pentecostal Holiness Church. Shanna and Brian lived in their house in Franklin Springs, Georgia next to the campus of Emmanuel College.

I resigned the Church again. Enis asked what we were going to do.

I said, "I don't know. I just know I am not going to call anybody at the District office or apply at any church. If God wants me to pastor, He has my phone number."

GOD OPENS ANOTHER DOOR

A couple of days later the phone rang. Mrs. Diane Tarver, the widow of a good friend of mine called me from the First Assembly of God in Blakely GA.

"Charles, this is Diane Tarver. Otha wanted me to call you and see if you would be interested in pastoring our Church. (Otha was on the board of the church.)

My thought was, "South Georgia again, I don't think so." The Lord said, "If you are not going to open any doors, don't close any."

With that, I said, "Well, I can't say I wouldn't be interested. I resigned my church two weeks ago."

"That's when Otha asked me to call you."

Enis said it would take a miracle for us to be able to move. We drove down and preached that week-end. As I met with the board I expressed doubts about accepting the position. The former pastors had lived in the small apartment that was a part of the building.

We had three small children plus Jodie was still at home. When I told them the minimum it would take for me to meet my obligations I felt sure that would remove me from the list of prospects.

It was more than twice the amount they were paying the former pastors. They just looked at each other, nodded and said ok.

Jodie had attended a cosmetology school and was a beautician. She was working in a shop in Commerce. She said, "I'm not moving down there. I have not lost anything in Blakely, Georgia.

Enis was working out her notice with her job. She and Jodie, Sonya and Tonya would drive down each week-end and then go home on Sunday evening. Jonathan and I stayed in the small apartment.

Jodie always had a boy-friend from the time I gave her permission to start dating. The boys were serious in their relationship with her. She moved down with the rest of the family. Some of the guys had courage to ask me for her hand in marriage.

Chris attended church with us in Commerce. When he asked me, I told him I was honored that he would want to marry my daughter and that I thought he was a fine young Christian man.

"However," I said, "it won't work. There is a special call on Jodie's life and she will not be happy until she fulfills that calling. I notice that you are content to not be so involved in ministry."

He came to Blakely that week-end. He said he had come to take her home with him to be his wife and that he could not follow her family around the country.

He said the next time he came down he was taking her home. She told him she could not go with him.

There were several young men who began to attend services with us. She told them she was not going to get emotionally involved with them. She was just going for the fellowship of the crowd.

One Sunday was set aside for Youth Sunday. Jodie did not tell me what she was going to do. I sat in the congregation and watched her as she stood and took on the role of the pastor. She was wearing one of my suits and talking like I talk by saying things I would say and how I would say them. Then she began to take off these clothes. I was in shock and about to stop this situation.

Enis took my arm and said, "It'll be alright. Just wait."

She was wearing another set of clothes. Once again, she did the same thing, and after about the forth set of clothes began talking to the youth like a youth leader should. I was shocked at her creativity.

As she began to minister to the youth of the Church, the youth department began to grow in number. The District Youth Leader from Macon called and asked her to be the Youth Rep for the Blakely section. It was time for the District Youth Convention to be held in Griffin, GA. She was asked to teach in one of the sessions.

Once again, her creativity kicked in. She had her Mother to make her a special dress with one sleeve. She painted a golden line down the center of her face. One side of her face was painted gold and the other side was without any make-up.

Her hair was styled one way on one side and another way on the other. She would walk across the front of the class room with the golden face showing and talk about how much fun they could have at the party.

Then she would walk back across the room and the other side would show as she talked about being sold out to God and letting God be their joy.

She did this presentation twice. Each time she made the statement that she was a bride in waiting. I haven't met him yet, but I know God has told me to wait.

During the lunch break we met Brian and Shanna for lunch at the front of the church.

Brian's friend Dewayne Creswell was there. He had been judging the musical talent at the youth function. For the first time, Jodie had no words. She was so quiet.

As we walked away, Dewayne asked Brian, "Is she taken?" Brian said no.

During Jodie's second session Brian came in and sat with me.

When she got to the part where she said, "God told me I was to be a bride in waiting. I haven't met him yet, but I know God has told me to wait."

Brian leaned over and said to me, "She doesn't know it, but she just met him while ago."

When I asked what he meant, he said, just wait and see. She and Dewayne are going to get married.

The next day the phone rang. "Hello," I said.

"Hello, sir. Is Jodie there?"

"Yes, she is."

"May I speak to her?"

I told Jodie I thought it was the young man she met in Griffin. She went into our bedroom, began to lay across the bed as she shut the door to answer the phone. I walked into the kitchen. The wall phone was right there. I picked it up in the middle of their conversation.

"Hey boy."

"Yes sir."

"If you are going to date my daughter you are going to have to change your shield."

"What do you mean, sir?"

"You are connected to the Congregational Holiness denomination aren't you?"

"Yes sir."

"Well I lost one daughter to the Pentecostal Holiness and that's as far down we are going. You are going to have to be Assemblies of God."

With that I hung up. He asked Jodie if her Daddy was serious. She said no, he is just crazy.

Let me say, that was done in fun. I have no negative feelings against either of these two denominations.

He began to come to see her. In a few months, they were married. I conducted the ceremony in our home church in Murrayville.

When we came to Blakely, the board had rented a house on Damascus Road about a mile from the Church for us. The home had belonged to a deceased elderly couple. It was apparent they had spent a lot of time taking care of their yard. When one shrub flower began to fade, another type of shrub flower began to bloom. The house set in a grove of tall pines.

Brother Otha Adkinson called as we were getting settled in and asked if we were home.

"I'm sending one of my men with some meat for you." The young man brought three tall freezer bags of fresh meat of all kinds. Our freezer never ran out. Brother Otha who owned the Blakely Freezer Locker loved and took care of his pastor. We were so grateful.

The church began to grow as we knocked on doors and invited people to come and be with us. We got a used school bus and began to pick people up and bring them to the services. We began a daily radio program that became popular.

I loved the town. I loved the people. I had a great board. Many days I would eat lunch with Brother Otha at the restaurant down the street from the house, "Miss B's." She cooked pies each day. Her food was always fresh and tasteful. The little restaurant set in a small grove of trees. She was a very sweet lady.

Sister Ruby McGowen was a very special and sweet lady. She was a very talented organist. She had married late in life to a great old time preacher. I learned later that he and his sister had been at Azua Street during that revival where the people were filled with the Holy Ghost and began to speak in tongues.

Sister Ruby had a problem with hearing. They would announce a page number and she would begin to play a different song. Often, they would stop and repeat the hymn number.

She thought she was mumbling to herself, but everyone could hear her when she would say, "I wish they would speak up."

She was diagnosed with cancer. One day I visited her in the local hospital and she began to tell me about the angels outside of her window that were talking. I knew the workers at the hospital sat outside of her window to take their smoke breaks.

When I walked in and spoke to her that morning, she asked me if I was not going to speak to Jesus.

I told her I had talked with Him that morning.

She said, "Well, He's standing right there. Don't you see Him?"

"No, ma'am, I don't see Him. I'm sorry." I knew what this meant. She was about to go home to be with Him. I called Enis and she came and stayed with her. I had left for a few minutes when Enis called and told me she was gone.

There are people that come along beside you as you walk down the road of life. Some are coming on while others are leaving you as you walk. Each one adds so much to our lives. Sister Ruby was one of those for me.

The Brunson's were another couple that we loved. They spent hours in their humble home playing dominoes. They were faithful to God and to the Church.

Brother Wallace Gordon and his wife were special as well. Wallace had always been a hard worker but was eventually diagnosed with cancer.

One day I was on a trip for Brother Otha and drove through Moultrie, Georgia. I came beside a pick up loaded with collard greens. I followed him to the farmer's market and asked about the price.

I went home, got my little trailer and Brother Wallace. We filled the trailer with collard greens. My objective was to give him something to do to make some money. We made a few stops to sell a few bundles of collard greens.

Then we came to a friend who was working on the roof of a house. I asked him if he wanted some collard greens. He asked the price and then how many did we have.

I told him and he said, "I'll take them." He paid us and then I took Brother Wallace home, gave him the money and went home. For me it was a great day.

All the people were just great. Ben and Sandra Cooper were special to us. She would find old stray and abandoned dogs in the country side and give them a great home. I can't tell you the times prayer requests were made for one of her dogs. We prayed and God answered.

One day she started out the front door of her house, but her dog would not allow her to open the door. She walked out the back door and came to the front door to find a very large rattle snake at her front door.

My golf partner didn't care that I couldn't play golf. He invited me to go with him. Brother Homer was a great man of God who played the guitar at Church. We played golf together but he warned me to not try to reprieve the golf ball from the little ponds. Alligators lived in those little ponds. You could get close and then see those eyes pop up to look at you.

Gwyn Weeks was a special lady. She came and helped Enis a number of times, but especially when we first moved into the house. She was good with wood-work. We have some items she made especially for us. I was invited back to perform the marriage for her daughter when she got married.

Brother Jimmy was on the board when we came. Later he began to preach and now he is a pastor in a local church. It is always good when you see ministry rise up from your congregation.

When I pastored in Bainbridge, Georgia, our Presbyter, Brother George Tarver pastored this Church. Many time I would drive up to spend some time with him to get his counsel.

George had cancer and passed away several years ago. It was his wife, Sister Diane Tarver that called me. She served on the board and was a very special friend to us. We loved her and her two children.

Brother Wallace had a brother named Sam. Sam and Wallace had a Godly Mother who prayed for them for years. I felt the Lord tell me it was time for a revival meeting, and that I was to call a good friend of mine, Evangelist Milton Martin, Jr. I called and found him in a meeting in Rome, Georgia.

I asked if he could come and hold the meetings for us. He came and spent most of his time during the day in prayer for the meeting.

One night at the close of the service he asked, "Is there a Samuel, Sammy, or Sam here? Somebody with the name of Sam, God has been dealing with me all day that He has a message for this person."

There was no response.

Then Wallace's sister stood and said, "I've got a brother named Sam."

"Tell him to be here tomorrow night. God's got a word for him."

Sam hauled logs. The first time I saw him was at his home. Wallace asked me to go with him to visit Sam. The second time I saw Sam he was in jail.

The next night Sam came to the meeting. At the close of the service the question was asked. "Is Sam here tonight?"

"Right here, Preacher," Sam said as he raised his one arm.

"Come on down here, Sam." Sam got up and walked down the aisle to the front of the Church.

"Sam," Milton said, "this doesn't make any sense to me, but God said the men on the street have been wondering where have you been for the past thirty years."

Then Milton placed his hand on each side of Sam's rib cage and began to pray forcibly. Sam raised his hand and began to pray.

Sam was the town drunk. He would drink a fifth of liquor for breakfast, get in his log truck and then drank another fifth of liquor before lunch.

Instantly God delivered Sam for this alcoholic addiction. The next week Sam went home and God baptized him in the Holy Spirit.

Sam told me, "Preacher, over thirty years ago, God called me to preach. I have been running from God ever since."

I asked him how he lost his arm. He said he was with another man's wife when the man came in and caught him. When the husband raised the shotgun, Sam ran around the wall. The blast cost him his arm.

Sam's life was changed. I had him preach for me several times and when he would go with me to other churches in the section I had him preach for me a few times then.

His preaching was like he was, rough and unpolished. His sincerity came through and it touched a lot of lives. Most of the people knew Sam, or knew of him. The transformation in his life was a testimony of the power of God to deliver.

Sam told me one day a young black man knocked on his door. When he opened the door, the young man pointed a loaded pistol at his head and said come and go with me.

"I told the young man I wasn't going anywhere with him. If he was going to shoot me, which was what he was planning to do, he would have to do it right there."

The young man pulled the trigger. The gun snapped. He pulled the trigger again, and again the gun snapped. The young man threw the gun down and ran away.

Sam said, "I picked the new pistol up and pulled the trigger as I pointed the gun to the ground. It fired. Preacher, I know God saved my life again. He must have something for me to do for Him.

It was during this time that I served as the Presbyter of the Blakely Section. We had a very good relationship with the other pastors and churches in the section.

There was a large house on the north side of the square. I presented the idea that to have a parsonage like this would be to their advantage when it was time to call a new pastor. The Board agreed and purchased the house.

One Wednesday evening I said, "It is impossible for anyone to steal from you if you just give the item to them in your mind." Enis was just shaking her head. After church, I asked her what that was all about.

She said, "I didn't know if you knew you had given somebody the radio out of Jonathan's car."

Once again it was time to move on. Some of the people were not happy that I did not keep office hours. My hours were spent out in the community witnessing to folks.

When I heard some of the ladies were having prayer meetings in their homes, I got the feeling they were trying to pray their pastor out. I went by the Freezer Locker and spoke to Brother Otha and told him I felt I should resign. The next Sunday I turned in my notice to the Church. There were those who were sad and there were those who showed no remorse.

These people are still my friends and I love them dearly. They know they can call me anytime, and they have from time to time.

NEW LIFE ASSEMBLY

We were contacted by a church from the Augusta area. Their pastor was ready to retire and they were looking for someone to come and replace her. It was a beautiful congregation. The music was moving and powerful. I preached that morning and then we spent the afternoon at the Pastor's house.

The next week we preached at a little struggling church in Cornelia. I felt the Lord say He would bless me either way, but that He needed me at the church in Cornelia. We pastored that church for a little over three years.

The youth pastor, Mark McIntyre came to me and said, "I guess you might want me to resign so you can get someone else to be the youth pastor."

"No, not at all, I'd like for us to work together. You have a good number of young people here that seem to love the Lord."

I met Mark's dad, Charlie McIntyre at a District Men's Rally at our campground in Forsyth, Georgia. He was singing with a quartet. I saw him again at the Church in Cornelia.

Charlie and I became very close friends in a very short time. He was such a likeable person, and that was a wonderful friendship that affected my life in many ways.

On one occasion, Mark said, "Pastor, when we promise the kids something, I don't want to disappoint them. I had that happen to me so many times in my former church."

"I agree with you. If there is any way possible we want to fulfill our promises to these kids," I said.

"I told them that if we raised a certain amount of money for missions we would take them to Daytona Beach, Florida for a week. My Daddy will drive us down in their bus. Because the air is not cold we will leave at midnight on Sunday and by the time we wake up, we will be there," Mark said.

That was the plan. That Sunday night the kids came to the church with their sleeping gear and suit cases. Excitement was in the air.

Then it happened.

Mark called me aside and said, "Pastor, we have a problem. Mama is sick with a virus and Daddy doesn't want to leave her until in the morning."

"I'm sorry. Well, I will just go home and sleep in my bed and see you in the morning."

The next morning the phone rang. "Pastor, we *really* have a problem. Daddy has gotten this virus. He said for you to come over and drive the bus."

Panic struck me. There is no way I could ever do that. It would be like driving the Titanic down a back alley. I could never do that!

I tried to find someone to drive his bus but without success. I tried to find someone who had a bus to drive and again no luck. I went to Charlie's house to check on him. Maybe he's feeling better now, I thought.

"Come on out here, Preacher. There's nothing to it." We got on the bus. He flipped the switch pressed the button and it started. He drove it out of the drive way and on to the main road.

Then he pulled over and said, "Now you try it."

It was a four-speed manual transmission vehicle. Reluctantly I sat in the driver's seat and started up the steep hill. When we arrived at the church, the kids began to load their luggage.

As we passed Gainesville I called my friend Bobby Smith and said, "You are not going to believe what I am doing. I don't even believe what I am doing! I am driving a big bus."

I drove to Daytona Beach. I exited the freeway and stopped at the light. I felt pretty good with such a smooth stop.

The light changed and I took my foot off the clutch but the clutch pedal stayed on the floor.

"What do I do now?" I thought.

I put my toe under the clutch pedal and lifted it up and revved up the engine. Tires squeaked as the bus jerked forward. I prayed for green lights at every intersection as I drove down the street to the hotel.

If I looked ahead and saw the traffic signal was red, I would slow down. If it was green, I would speed up. We made it. That was a miracle. The next morning Charlie came to the hotel. He was really looking good as far as I was concerned.

Another time we took the youth to the "Lost Sea Caves" in Tennessee. That was an amazing trip. We slept in the cave with other youth groups.

If you think people snore loud in your home, you should hear it in a large cave! We got so muddy sliding down those little paths. The fish in the lake had no eyes. Because of the gross darkness they did not need eyes to see. Their other senses were strengthened to adapt to their circumstances.

Mark and his wife Becky had been married a few years and it seemed they could not have children. One Sunday she came forward for prayer. A short time later they were expecting their first child.

Mark worked a full-time job, went to college full time and served as our youth pastor. When Becky had complications and the doctors told her to stay in bed, Mark had to change his schedule.

He asked me if the church could help them with fifty dollars a week. I made a grave mistake by presenting the proposal to the Church. A lady in the back said she thought that was a bad idea.

"The next thing you will want to start paying the piano player."

I began to give him some money each week for a short time.

Later he came to me and said he would have to give up his position as the youth pastor. I hated to see him go. This young man was special. He was not satisfied to just get by. He had a 4.0 grade average even with his schedule and duties. God blessed him with his own business.

Some years later Mark and Becky came to see us during the Christmas season. He asked me to go for a ride with him. We rode and talked while Becky visited Enis. When we returned to my house he gave me an envelope as a Christmas gift. It contained several hundred dollars.

After he left, the group of young people began to diminish. No one understood the "New Life" that was evidenced in the lives of the young people. Even today I occasionally see some of those kids. Most of them are still living for the Lord.

It wasn't long until I resigned.

Eventually the church closed. The second Sunday after we left, the District sold the building to a Hispanic congregation.

THE BUS, A NEW MINISTRY

About the time New Life Assembly of God began to struggle financially, Tempe Brown came to see us and told us her son owned a bus company in Kennesaw and was looking for drivers. I applied for the job to help our income.

I had no experience except for the first voyage with our youth. Tommy Brown became a good friend. My first trip was to ride with him to take a group to Rock Eagle. On the way back, he had me drive.

I worked for him for several years. During that time, I made several mistakes, but he was patient with me.

I picked up a group of Georgia Alumni on Peachtree Street in Atlanta and took them to the Georgia-South Carolina game in Columbia, South Carolina. It seemed Interstate 20 would never end.

I left early that morning, drove to Kennesaw which was 98 miles from my house, got the bus and made the pick-up. There was more booze on that bus than most beer trucks.

I thought, "What in the world am I doing with this group of people." Little did I know that God was about to do something great.

We got to the field as the sun was going down. We came up to the field turned right and drove past the warehouses on both sides of the street. The further I went down the hill with the bus, the darker it became. I was now driving in the shadow of the darkness. It was the darkest as I parked at the end of the warehouse.

This was in an old cotton mill village. There was no good place to park this large bus. I turned right and pulled in behind one of the warehouses opened the bay doors and they had their tail-gate party. I sat on the bus.

They left the bus and went to the game.

I got my Bible and began to review my sermon notes for the next morning. The sermon title was, "He Went Farther." It was about Jesus going past the Inn to the stable to be born, going past the disciples in the Garden to pray, and at death He not only went to the grave, He went farther to walk out of that tomb. Then, at the ascension, as they watched, He went farther.

The Spirit of God was strong as I studied that evening. It began to get late. I wondered what was going on in the game.

I got out of the bus and walked across the parking lot. Two couples were nearby, standing near their car and grilling chicken.

"What's the score?" I asked.

"Georgia is 17 and South Carolina is 3. Where did you come from?"

"Man, I just came from the presence of the Lord!" I don't know why I said that except I felt the anointing of the Spirit of God on me so strong.

"Are you a preacher," the young man asked.

"Yes, I am."

"Then I want to ask you a question. Why did God kill my daddy with cancer?"

"Well, I have the answer. You may not like it, but I have the answer. John 10:10 says, 'The thief cometh not, but for to steal, and to kill, and to destroy: I am come that they might have life, and that they might have it more abundantly.' God did not kill your daddy. Satan did. Killing is not God's doing. That is the devil's delight. When the devil told God he was going to kill your Daddy, God said, I don't think so. I am going to give him eternal life."

"Right now, your Daddy is standing just inside the gate. He hears the beautiful singing. He is looking down the golden avenue to the celebration and he so wants to be there, but he can't move from where he is because you won't let him go. You need to give him permission to go and enjoy the good things God has prepared for him."

It was at this point I shared the story of Dan and Bobbi Hale. Dan called me that Sunday afternoon and said Bobbi, his wife who had cancer, had gone home to be with the Lord that morning.

She got up, made breakfast and then friends came by on the way to church.

They sat and talked about the fond memories. When they left, she told Dan she was tired and was going to lie down. He said that was alright and that he would be in there after he finished doing the dishes and cleaning the kitchen.

"When I went into the room," he said, "she was gone. I held her in my arms and said Bobbi; you cannot leave me like this. You have to come back! It seemed like fifteen minutes, he said, but I know it was well over five minutes."

She opened her eyes and said, "Dan, please let me go. It is so beautiful there."

Dan continued, "I kissed her good bye and told her to go and enjoy what God had for her. She closed her eyes and slipped away."

I asked permission to pray for this man and his wife and friends. He said ok. I prayed and walked back into the shadows toward the bus.

When I got on the bus, the anointing was so strong.

I felt God say, "That was good. Now go back and get his name and address and phone number. I want you to follow up on him."

I made my way back through the maze of cars in the darkness and come up behind their car again. They were talking a mile and minute and did not see me coming.

"I'm sorry to bother you again." Startled they turned and looked as if they had seen a ghost.

"Are you an angel? Where did you come from, where did you go?"

"No, I am not an angel. I am driving a charter bus and brought some alumni from Georgia here for the game."

Then I asked the young man directly, "Am I hearing you right? Are you telling me that you don't want to have anything to do with the God who gave your father eternal life, but you would rather serve the deceitful Satan that killed him?"

He paused and then said, "I guess that is what I have been saying, isn't it?"

"Wouldn't you rather serve the God who gave him eternal life so you can be there with him throughout eternity rather than miss him while he is there and you are in hell?"

"Yes, I would."

He and his wife asked Jesus to come into their hearts and lives. They bowed their heads and with cans of beer in their hands prayed sincerely.

When I called him a few weeks later, they had gone back to church and made a public confession of the saving power of Jesus. The last I heard, he was teaching a Sunday school class for junior boys.

When I questioned why I was there, the question comes back to me what if I had not been there.

On another occasion, I took a church group from LaGrange, Georgia to the ski slopes in West Virginia. They requested that I take them to the slopes first instead of going to the motel. I left them and drove back to the motel with the understanding that I would pick them up later that evening.

I was sharing with the motel clerk about the Lord and His love for us. She asked for prayer about some situations in her family.

About that time a taxi pulled up. It was a young couple and their child and a grandfather and his granddaughter. I told them they should have called me, that I would have returned and picked them up and brought them to the motel.

I was about to get some supper and asked them if they wanted to join me. Then I was going to the ski slopes and pick up the rest of the group. They said they would join me.

As we sat at the table I began to talk about the Lord and His goodness and His love for us. Mike, the young father said he would like to hear me preach sometime. "Well, come by the room when we get back and I'll share some things with you."

We made the trip to the slopes, got the rest of the group and came back to the motel. Mike and his wife and child came to my room. I shared about Abraham when he was about to sacrifice his son, Isaac.

God called out to Abraham at the critical moment, "Abraham," Abraham replied, "Behold, here I am." Then God said, "Do the lad no harm."

Abraham was a friend of God. But God had another friend in the past. That was Adam. We don't know how long God and Adam walked in the garden each evening.

But, one day God came into the garden and called out to His friend, "Adam." God waited but there was no answer. He called again, "Adam." Again, there was no answer. Then God in His search for His friend said, "Adam, where are you?"

Adam came to face God. He said, "I heard your voice in the garden and I ran and hid myself because I was naked."

Then I asked Mike, "If God were to call you today, Mike, would you say like Abraham, "Behold, here I am, or would you be like Adam and say I was hid among the stuff You gave me?"

Mike turned to his wife and son and asked them to go on to the room assuring them he would be coming soon. As they walked out the door he said, "Preacher, I'm afraid I would have to say I have been hid among the stuff. I don't want to be that way."

His prayer was sincere as I led him in what we call the sinner's prayer.

A few months later as Enis and I were on our way to Columbus, GA, I called Mike.

His wife answered the phone. "Hello."

"Is Mike there?" There was silence for a brief time and in a quiet voice she asked, "Is this the bus driver?"

"Yes, it is."

"I'm sorry to tell you Mike died three weeks ago."

What if I had not been there for that critical meeting in Mike's life? What if even though I was there, I had not shared about God? The door of opportunity to speak to him about eternal things would have been missed.

As you read this, ask yourself, are you talking to others about the God you know? Are you sharing with others the good things He has done in your life and the lives of your family and friends?

BARROW WORSHIP CENTER

During this time, a dear minister friend and his wife that had been worshipping with us in Cornelia left to preach at the Winder Assembly of God. He was to just fill in until they got a pastor, but he said he felt God had called him to pastor that church.

The Church was meeting in the old BPOE lodge building next door to a car dealership. Brother Baird sold the property and bought some acreage a few miles down the street.

With the proceeds, the church built the metal building debt free. The property had a house that could be used as a parsonage.

He had asked me to come and be the music minster but I did not feel I was to do that. When he resigned, he had a pastor from a neighboring Baptist Church to be the next pastor. I was asked to come and preach for three weeks as the new pastor took some time off. When he came back after a few weeks, that pastor resigned.

The Presbyter asked me what I thought about pastoring that church.

I said, "No thanks. That Church is a dream killer. So many have come and only stayed for a short time. It would be like buying an expensive ticket on a parked bus. You aren't going anywhere."

But, we came and served as pastor of this Church for eleven years. I learned that three ladies would meet every Tuesday morning for prayer. They would pray for God to not let their Church close. That moved me. We saw God do some great things in this time. The Church grew. Lives were changed.

One day my friend, Bobby Smith came to see me. Bobby had been the young boy who asked the question "who is this Jesus feller, anyway?"

He was having a difficult time with his business. Eventually he lost his business and his home. I went to see him and asked him what his plans were. He said he did not know.

I said, "Why don't you come and help me. I can't promise a lot, but we have a parsonage you can live in and we will take care of the utilities and perhaps we can pay a little each week as we are able."

After a few days, he called me and asked if the offer still stood. I said yes and they began to move in. He worked with the youth. The group began to grow.

Bobby is a master mechanic and can do anything. He took care of the building, fixed the cars of the parishioners, served as my right-hand man.

Each Monday morning, we had our staff meeting. He was always there. Together the ministry grew and so did we.

Since I was not excited about taking the church, I confess that I had a bad attitude in the early days. I thought that if they ever got to where they could not pay me, I promised myself that I would leave.

One Sunday the secretary said, "Pastor, I am sorry to tell you that we don't have the funds to pay you."

For some reason, I had peace. I didn't hear the Lord speak to me. It was as if I already knew the answer. The message was, "That's ok. I've got this."

I had no idea what that meant.

Monday morning, I got a call from Mark McIntyre, my former youth pastor, "Pastor, could you and Sister Enis meet Becky and me for lunch tomorrow?"

The next day we met at the restaurant in Cornelia. When we walked back to our cars as he opened his car door he said, "Becky and I want to bless you and Sister Reese, and your church." He gave me two checks. One was made out to the Church and one was made out to me. They were each for two thousand five hundred dollars.

I have often said walking by faith was wonderful and then added, "When it's over."

This was another time when God showed the power of His faithfulness.

One Sunday evening Pastor Bobby preached a good message. I was so ready to get a word from God. He began to speak to my heart about a ship. This is what He said.

THE SHIP

Barrow Worship Center in Winder, Georgia has just had its fifty-year celebration. The Celebration was in good taste. The objective was to give honor to all the former pastors and glory to God.

There was a long list of former pastors with most of them staying less than eighteen months. To some looking from the outside, the church had been viewed as having little or no real significance to the Kingdom of God.

That is not to say that there were no souls saved or lives changed. There are those who could testify to that. However, the Church has for the most part had an attendance of 50 or less down through these 50 years with an occasional bump up to 60 or 70.

It was said in a Sunday night service that it was time for this Church to grow up and step up to its place that God has ordained. As we were in the altars that night, God began to deal with me.

I saw an old ship, like the Mayflower or one of that vintage, moored in the docks.

The thought came that I have been busy trying to fill the ship, with crew and passengers.

I hadn't paid attention to the main thing, and that was, "What is this Ship's destination." If the ship is going to the right destination, people will line up to get on board.

They will even pay to get on board, and the crew will feel honored to serve.

As I thought on this, I realized I did not know our destination. I see some ports of call along the way. But none of these are our destination.

We see many churches sailing along. Some are going in the same direction we are going while others are sailing in the opposite direction. There are some sailing to our left while others are sailing to our right. We are sailing because that is what we do. Sunday after Sunday, we sail.

We don't know if we are making any progress on our journey if we don't know where we are going. We could sail east for a while, and then on a whim, turn and sail west. It seems to make no difference.

We are applauded because of our sailing abilities. Is there no one asking the all-important question? Does it not make any difference for anyone? Where are we going? That is a question every church needs to answer.

For me, anytime I find myself on a long journey, my mind shortens the journey by breaking it up into segments. When I reach point B, I am moving closer to point C. Someone said that if you will go as far as you see, you will see farther.

Where are we going?! God is showing me just a little at a time. I have discovered that while I may be the captain of this ship, He is the Admiral of the fleet. I must receive my orders from Him. He knows the beginning from the end.

In His unlimited knowledge, He has been there before. Like sheep following the shepherd, just follow where He leads. He knows where the water and the green grass is located.

Where do I want this Ship to go? I want us to become a strong vibrant ship. We may feel so small out on the Sea of Time, but when we pull into the ports, we should have grown to the point that our size will dwarf the docks. Dwarfing the docks and other sailing vessels is not our objective. Our objective is way beyond that. We must grow to the task given us by the Admiral of this fleet.

Often the attendance of a church remains small because those that call this their home do not see the need to faithfully attend regularly. Therefore, they do not support their Church regularly financially. The greater the value of a thing, the more we care.

But, it is not a heavy burden because we do it unto Jesus. I believe that church membership does not carry the weight it should when the member does not see its value. Could it be that it is because no one has emphasized the destiny of the Ship?

How would you like to get on a ship that will carry you to total deliverance? This Ship can go safely through the straits of "Sinful Living" to Salvation through the Blood of Jesus.

It can lead you through the dungeons of life to the freedom you desire. Whom the Son sets free is free indeed. Your chains will fall off and you will experience that freedom.

THE STROKE

One day a neighboring pastor was asking about our two churches merging. I called for the District Superintendent, Brother Rick Collins to come and meet with us. After the meeting, he had dinner with Enis and me before he was to leave.

He asked how long had it been since I had had a sabbatical. I told him I had never had a sabbatical.

He said, "I want you and your wife to take the month of November off. I will give you one thousand dollars, and take care of the Church while you are gone."

I was to do no preaching during the sabbatical.

I have a second cousin who owned a house on the beach at Panama City Beach. I asked her about the use of the house. She said there would be no charge since this was not the busy season.

On Thursday evening, in November 2011, we had the sectional Light for the Lost Missions Banquet which I attended.

Also, I had to conduct the funeral of a grandmother of one of our parishioners. Friday, we went to see Enis's brother Roger and his wife and spent some time with them.

That Sunday morning, we visited the small Methodist Church in our neighborhood, Mt. Pleasant. We had lunch with them and then drove to Columbus, Georgia and had dinner with our son Jonathan and his family. Then we spent the night with our daughter Jodie and her family.

It was the eleventh of November, 2011 when we got out of town and started toward Panama City Beach. We stopped in Dothan, Alabama and visited a couple that used to be in the church in Commerce. Then we headed down the road.

Enis and I were having disagreements. It seemed that whatever decision I made, she would dispute it. There were some hard things said both by me and by her. I was hurting. I never thought I would ever be interested in getting a divorce, but I was there. This was Saturday night.

She said, "I feel as if I have lost you."

"You have. You have hurt me so deeply that I am ready to call it quits."

We drove on in silence. Coming through town we saw a church that I thought we might attend in the morning. We got up got dressed and went to church. Afterward we had lunch at a local Olive Garden and went to the cottage. We took our naps in separate rooms.

When we got up we sat and talked about what was going on between us. A peace came over us. It seemed like the calm after the storm had passed.

The next morning the plan was to walk to the porch onto the sand and down to the edge of the water. I wanted to sit and listen to the waves in an effort to hear from God. We got up, took our showers and began to get dressed. I turned and saw Enis lying on the bed. Her face was contorted and she could not speak. I realized this was real.

SHE WAS HAVING A STROKE!

I called Jodie and told her, "Your Mother is having a stroke!"

"Daddy call 911 right away! Time is of the essence. I am on my way."

I called 911 and tried to get Enis dressed before they got there. Meanwhile Jodie had called Shanna, Jonathan, Sonya and Tonya.

The fire truck came and then the ambulance. They took her to the hospital, but where is the hospital? I had no idea. I had to go through Enis's pocket book and see if I could find her Medicare card, driver's license and any other papers I would need.

I began to drive back into Panama City looking for signs for the hospital. I finally found the hospital and there was only one parking space. The sign said, "Doctors only." I pulled in and got out of the car.

A man said kindly, "Sir you can't park there. That is for doctors only."

I said, "I don't care who it's for. My wife has had a stroke and I am going in to check on her!"

"Sir, if you will give me your keys, I will park your car for you."

I gave him the keys, got the valet parking stub, rushed into the hospital building and found her in the room where they were trying to intubate her. They were struggling and I knew they were not being successful. They put the tube into her esophagus instead of her trachea. She was blown up like a balloon because the air was filling the tissues of her skin.

They moved her to the ICU. Her left lung had collapsed. The stroke was on the right side and her side was paralyzed. She could not speak. Because her INR was high they decided to not give her a shot that would break up the blood clot that they thought was causing the stroke.

They put a tube in the left side of her chest because that lung had collapsed.

The doctor said, "Mr. Reese, if she lives through the night, and I don't think she will, she will be just a vegetable."

"Thank you, doctor, but I cannot accept that."

Jodie and Jonathan drove down together and Shanna was right behind them. The second day began early as we went to the hospital. The doctors and nurses were working on her constantly.

We found a small private room and waited. Jodie stepped out for a minute and when she returned she said we needed to come to the waiting room across the hall.

There was a group of Pentecostal Christians there praying for some of their friends that had been admitted. When we walked in Jodie explained to them who we were and why we were there. They invited us to come and allow them to pray for us as they gathered around.

I knelt in the floor.

Someone touched my right leg.

It was a little boy praying beside his Daddy for me.

Afterward one of the men opened his wallet and gave me two one hundred dollar bills as he said he believed the Lord told him to do this. I graciously received the gift even though I had some money. I didn't know what the next few days would bring. I knew God knew and so I received the money as from Him.

Tuesday, November the fifteenth, I heard myself saying over and over, "I just can't believe this is happening, I just can't believe this is happening."

The doctors and nurses were very patient with all of us as we had an endless stream of questions. They took their time and answered each of us.

Enis had been heavily sedated. I held her hand and talked to her. Each of us took turns.

She did not respond. The nurses gave her constant care. Everybody was so patient and professional.

The phone rang constantly with folks wanting to know how she was doing. My friend Mark McIntyre called and I explained the situation to him.

Later his wife, Becky called. "Is there anything we can do for you?" she asked.

Their company was paying me to be a consultant. I asked if she would deposit the check in the bank for me and just pray. A few hours later Mark called again and said he was on his way to be with me.

When he got there, we went to get something to eat. He handed me some cash and said the check that was to be deposited into my account would be twice the regular amount. As he was leaving to go to his motel I began to thank God again for such wonderful caring friends as this family has been.

This Wednesday began early. Shanna and Jonathan did their morning run down the beach and then to the local mall. Jodie and I walked out the back door, off the porch onto the sand and found ourselves sitting as the water lapped at our feet. Our hearts were heavy.

I wondered how Enis did during the night.

I told Jodie that we could not allow ourselves to get depressed about this because we have to be strong for her sake.

We had to exercise our faith and keep it strong. It had to be "bulldog faith." The kind that says, "I'll not let You go until you bless me."

We gathered together, ate breakfast and made our way to the hospital. I took my guitar so I could sing to her, hoping the nurses would allow me to do that.

Enis was lying there. There was the breathing tube in her mouth, the IV's in her arms, and a tube in her left side to help her collapsed lung. There was no movement, no response from her at all. My soul cried out to God as I once again took her hand. This cry was deep, but had no sound.

There were no words except, "Oh God, please help us."

Shanna said, "I don't believe Mama is in there."

She began to talk about Mama being in heaven with her new body as she teared up.

Jonathan walked over after some time and took her hand.

"Mama, if you are in there we need you to let us know. If you are taking a tour and are planning on staying, that's fine, but you are going to have to come back and tell me."

After a few hours, she opened her eyes but there was a little response. She looked at us and her eyes began to follow us as we moved about the room.

We closed in around her bed and began to softly sing to her.

I asked her if she sung with us. There was a slight movement that said no. That let us know that she was still with us. God was working in the beginning of her healing.

Tonya called checking on her Mother. That evening she and Sonya arrived. They were shocked as they saw their Mother for the first time in that condition.

Thursday morning, I awoke at 3:30AM and could not go back to sleep. I got up at five.

Once again Shanna and Jonathan did their morning run down the beach and then through the local mall.

When we got to the hospital, Enis was opening her eyes more. Because of her body swelling, I had removed her wedding rings to prevent any complications they might cause. Jodie put them on her hand. Jodie walked up to the bed and showed Enis that she was wearing her rings.

Enis frowned and raised her left hand pointing with her ring finger, an indication that she did not want her rings removed from her hand.

Jodie posted on facebook, "That's the first time I have seen my Mama mad and I am glad." We were so glad for the response.

The prognosis was that she would not be able to process information, but she proved them wrong.

A very dear friend from our former church in Bainbridge came with his son to check on us.

Brother Orris Smith's friendship remained strong through the years. His son Lewis drove him down to see us. They had lunch with us and then returned home.

Mark came by and checked on us before he began his journey home. The rest of our family began to gather. My youth pastor, Bobby, called every day for an update.

The people of our Church were praying for us and rejoiced with us over every bit of progress. It was the little things in our lives that we never noticed that now seemed to hold the miracle for us.

Friday, November the eighteenth began. I came here to hear from God.

I have begun to sense that this was a, "Listen and you will hear Him, watch and you will see Him." day. He is working with us in our minds.

Sonya and Tonya came by and spent some time with Enis before they left to return home.

This hospital is the best one I have ever seen. The doctors and nurses are very professional, friendly and helpful. I learned they have valet parking for everyone that visits and there is no charge.

Enis was scheduled to get some medication the next day that would stimulate her and cause her to be more alert. That promised to be good for her. The phone calls continue from people who really care and know how to pray.

Pastor, Jeff Scalff of Saint Andrews Assembly of God came by and had prayer. For me it was good to have someone local to open their heart to us when we were in a strange place.

The nursing staff would come into the room as I would play the guitar and sing songs to Enis.

Psalm 89:1 says:

"I will sing of the mercies of the LORD
forever: with my mouth will I make
known thy faithfulness to all generations."

I was reading this to Enis and said, "Do you hear that? We are going to sing together again. So you can just get over this. We have got some singing to do."

There is another story in the Bible that I read to her. In I Samuel 27 we have the beginning story of David in a little city named Ziklag. In chapter 30 the story reminded me of Enis's situation.

David was running for his life. Nothing indicates a relationship with his brothers or his parents. He is now living at the graciousness of the Philistines.

An enemy came while David and his six hundred men were out to fight for the Philistines and burned the town, took their wives and children, their cattle and all that they had.

The six hundred men were now angry with David and were about to kill him. He had no one to turn to. There was no help.

That was what I was seeing for Enis. She was locked inside of herself. She was unable to move or communicate. I am sure there were a lot of things she wanted to say, but was totally unable.

There may be times when in each of our lives we face similar circumstances. How did David get out of this situation? We know he did because later he became king.

The Bible says he did two important things. These are the keys to any dilemma you may find yourself in. First of all, he encouraged himself in the Lord. Read that line again until you get it!

I asked Enis, "How do you suppose he encouraged himself?"

She looked at me and waited for the answer. "Perhaps he began to remember those days out on the hillside with the sheep when he took his small home-made harp and sang love songs to God. He remembered how it felt to be in the presence of God.

He remembered the day when one of his little sheep cried out for help.

Something extraordinary came over David as he ran toward the lion that had the little lamb in its teeth. He without thinking of the dangers he was putting himself in grabbed that lion and ripped his jaws and rescued the little lamb.

What was it that gave him that strength that he did not know he had? It was his God.

Another time a bear came to destroy one of his lambs and again that same anointing of God came upon him and again, the life of the lamb was spared.

Perhaps he remembered the day the preacher came by and announced before his brothers and his parents that this runt of the family would one day be the king. That meant that this situation was not his destiny. There was more to come."

The second thing David did was to get a word from God. That was so very important to David, and that is so very important to me and you. David asked God if he should go after the enemy that had burned the town and kidnapped his family. God said yes, go and I will give you the victory.

"Did you hear that, honey? Victory was promised. But you can't have victory without having a battle. You have got to fight this thing. Don't give in and don't give up. Victory is assured. And," I added, "God said He would restore everything. I believe He is going to restore you completely."

There were days when oppression set in. I questioned what I was seeing. Is this Enis, my wife, or is this Enis the little girl. My heart sank. I felt the crushing pressure of the oppression.

I began to cry out to God.

My body was so tired after all this time without true rest. I was tired in body and in spirit and mind. Sunday morning, I woke up at three-thirty again. I got up and then went back to bed. I lay there under the heavy pressure. I wanted to go to church but knew my body was screaming for rest.

I got up, took a shower and got dressed. Jodie came into my room and lay across the bed. She began to share words of encouragement.

I sat a while and watched John Hagee on TV. His message was for me this time. My soul and spirit was so dry and thirsty. I really needed a word from God. I got up, fixed a sandwich and went to the hospital.

Enis opened her eyes as I quietly walked up to the side of her bed. I was struggling with the gown the staff gave me to wear. "I think I'm going to need some help to tie this gown," I said.

She reached for my hand and pulled me close. Then she reached for my lapel and began to pull the gown up on my shoulders. It was then that I knew my fears were unwarranted.

She slept most of the day. I sat in the chair as I watched her breathe and then took a nap.

Monday morning Jodie rode with me to the hospital. As we got off the elevator we were met by Dr. Julie Wauters the neurological doctor.

She said, "I have been waiting for you. You have got to see this. This has made my day!"

We walked into the room. Enis had been cleaned up and was lying on the bed with a big smile. The intubation tube had been removed. She had a smile from ear to ear.

Her eyes were wide opened and she was alert. She looked like a child at Christmas. She was so excited. I cried and I laughed and I cried and I laughed praising God. I asked her if she could speak. She nodded her head yes.

Then slowly she raised her eye brows and said, "WELL."

Again, I laughed and I cried and I laughed and I cried again praising God.

Later she began saying, "Yeah, oh well, you."

As hard as this was on me and the family, it had to be really tough on her. I called Shanna. She was on her way back to Panama City.

I said, "Your Mama wants to talk to you."

"Are you kidding me," she asked

I put the phone to Enis's ear. Her eyes were wide open and she was smiling so big. She began to nod her head yes, raise her eye brows and say over and over, "YEAH."

The Friday after Thanksgiving, Shanna and Evan were there with me. Jodie and Jonathan had gone to their respective homes for Thanksgiving with their families. Every day we saw another little miracle.

There was something she could do today that she could not do yesterday.

Later, Jonathan and his family arrived. The kids came to the door of the ICU room and waved at Grandma. She had begun eating by mouth. The feeding tube had been removed and now she was eating a few bites as they were watching to see how well she was able to swallow.

I left to spend some time on the beach with Jonathan's children. Before I left I took her hand and began to sing a few lines of a love song, "I love you," then she sang the next line with me, "You love me." It was the Barney song.

This is when I learned that our speech comes from the left side of our brain and our singing comes from the right side of our brain. When you can't say it, you can sing it. God was smart to create us with this back-up system.

Sunday after church I came to the hospital. The nurse asked me if I had talked to someone about taking Enis to Warm Springs, Georgia to the Roosevelt Rehabilitation Center. I had been scheduled to take Enis there.

I was given permission to let her lie down in the back seat of the car and drive her there instead of using an ambulance. I called Bobby and asked him to drive my Cadillac down so she could have more room in the back seat.

He and his daughter, Rebecca came down Monday evening. I met them out front at the hospital. We ate dinner and drove to the beach house and he and I went back to the hospital.

Tuesday morning, we were scheduled to leave at 8 AM, but it was 11:15 before we were able to get out of there.

She was still on the air mattress that was on her bed. It took four strong men to get her in the back seat. Bobby followed me in the small car as I drove her to the hospital in Warm Springs. We stopped only twice. We were about five miles away when I got a call. It was their nurse asking if we were coming.

"I am just outside of town. You will need about four strong men and a gurney to get her out of this car."

When I got there, two staff ladies and a wheel chair awaited us.

"Come on Mrs. Reese, we got you, honey. You are alright. You're sitting in the chair now. We are going to take you to your room and give you a shower and get you ready to rest."

Enis's eyes were wide open as these two ladies got her out of the car. I think the look on her face read, "They are going to drop me."

It took all of ten seconds for the transfer. They wheeled her to her room as I parked the car and walked into the admissions office.

They gave her a shower, washed her hair and got her ready for bed. Enis looked refreshed and was glad to be able to get back in bed. I left and went to Jodie's nearby home for the night.

The next morning, I arrived at the hospital. Enis was sitting in the wheel chair. They had her in rehab working with her.

On December first as I went into the hospital I saw Enis feeding herself. Such a simple thing any other time, but this was a miracle for the "vegetable" the doctor said she would be. The therapy seemed such little techniques, but brought great results. On December third, during rehab she stood up. That was another miracle.

I brought her home on December twentieth. Bobby's Grandmother had passed away during this time. She had been in her hospital bed and was living with Bobby's Mother. Bobby brought the bed to our house, moved the furniture out of the dining room and set the bed up.

Because the stairs were so close to the door and Enis was now in the wheel chair, he came and modified our stair case to allow the wheel chair to pass. He installed handicap handles around the commode in the bath room.

I thank God for this dear true friend

I had to wake up every two hours and turn her over in the bed to keep her from having bed sores. We placed the little red bell beside her bed for her to ring when she needed me. I would raise her up on the bed, use the little board to move her over to the wheel chair, take her to the bath room, do the paper work and then move her back to the bed.

Therapists came to our house and as they worked with her she made progress each day.

My life had changed drastically. One day I had about gone what I thought was my limit when Jodie came to stay with her Mother for a while. She told me to just get away for a few hours.

While driving down the road I turned on the radio. A country song was playing. I had never heard this song before, but the singer said he and his wife were not getting along. They had had a few words. He went out to the barn to feel sorry for himself when he met an old man.

The old man said, "Son you should get on your knees and thank your lucky stars you still have her. You don't know lonely until you see it written in stone."

It seemed God had my number and knew exactly what I needed to hear as He delivered it to me over the radio.

Over the next weeks, the therapists taught her how to get in and out of the bed, how to stand, how to walk.

Each day brought a new step toward that total healing. Enis was fighting the fight the best she knew how looking for that complete victory.

We searched for out-patient therapy places and finally settled on a place in Gainesville. She had physical therapy, speech therapy, and occupational therapy. She was taught how to walk up and down stairs. The congregation saw her the first time she walked down the aisle to the front row of the church and sat down.

One evening at one of our board meetings she attended with me we were closing in prayer and I saw her begin to move her thumb on her right hand. Now she is able to raise her hands as she praises the Lord, and she can clap.

RETIREMENT

The Church was patient with our physical circumstances. Bobby was a blessing to us in filling in where ever needed, from maintenance to preaching. He had begun to sing with the gospel group he had sung with before.

I asked if he was ready to become pastor of the Church. He said he felt that was what he was supposed to do, but it was up to me. I told him to get ready because I was going to announce my retirement soon.

In the board meeting that evening after the other business on the agenda I shared with them that I felt it was time for the Church to, "Change gears."

I felt we had brought the Church a long way and had had a degree of success, but it was time for a change. I told them God had the answer in the house. Bobby was ready, qualified and felt the call to take the helm. "I would like to submit his name as a candidate to be your next pastor."

They discussed it and it was unanimous. The board would present his name before the Church to be voted on. It was overwhelmingly, "yes."

That last Sunday morning in October marked our eleventh year serving Barrow Worship Center. The Church was packed.

At the close of the sermon, I called for our new Pastor, Bobby and his wife, Ruby to come to the front. I gave him the charge to watch over the flock of God's people. Then I placed the mantle on his shoulders, gave him a new Bible, and had prayer from them and the Church and then presented the new pastor and his wife to the Church.

Today the Church is growing. They are seeing souls making decisions for Jesus, they are baptizing them and they are being added to the Church like the Bible commands. I am very proud of this young man that at an early age once jumped off the top of the porch to be with me.

50TH ANNIVERSARY

On March 20, 2015, Enis and I celebrated our 50th wedding anniversary. Our home Church in Murrayville graciously opened their doors and hearts to us. Jodie, who is now a wedding planner in the Columbus area, decorates for these weddings came. She and Shanna and some of our grandchildren decorated the Church beautifully. Pastor John Raburn officiated.

Once again, the house was packed. Our family and friends came from all over to help us celebrate. Enis has said to me many times, "I have always loved you, but I haven't always liked you."

Of course, I agree with that. I have had times when I didn't like me either. But when I was thinking about us, I wrote these words.

IT'S JUST ME AND YOU

Two lonely young hearts met in a crowded room
Timid and shy, I couldn't let the chance go by
For somehow in my heart I knew as they turned out the light,
We must have been a sight, for it was just me and you.
As time went on we dated a while
You won me over with your sweet voice and tender smile

You were different, somehow from the others I knew
I asked you to be mine until the end of time
And for the rest of our lives, it was to be just me and you.

Some of our times have been long and tough
But there have been more times when we've had plenty.
Times when we had friends, and times when we didn't have
any
But, in this world filled with deceit,
One thing has always been true.
Each night, when we turned out the light, it's just me and
you.

"Will you love me in years to come?
Once, I heard you say."
I answered, "I don't know about tomorrow, Honey,
But I love you today.

We've had our share of sunshine and rain,
Cups of joy, and troubles too.
Just as each day has come, it has also passed,
But it's still just me and you.

Well, it's been fifty years since we've said, "I do."
If I had known what I know now, way back then,
Without any hesitation on my part, I would do it all again.
We've been blessed with family and friends,
And there are many, not just a few.
But when they are all gone, and we are alone,
It will be just me and you.

THAT THEY MAY KNOW THERE IS A GOD IN ISRAEL

Many times, we have seen God intervene to save the lives of my family members. The following situations I share with you to let you know that God is a keeper of His word, and to tell you of the wonderful keeping power of our God. I am writing this chapter because I want my family to remember and not forget that God is not only faithful but He is powerful on our behalf.

In 1Samuel 17:45-46 we read these words,

> *"Then said David to the Philistine, Thou come*
> *to me with a sword, and with a spear, and*
> *with a shield: but I come to thee in the name*
> *of the LORD of hosts, the God of the*
> *armies of Israel, whom thou hast defied.*
> *This day will the LORD deliver thee*
> *into mine hand; and I will smite thee,*
> *and take thine head from thee; and I*
> *will give the carcasses of the host of*
> *the Philistines this day unto the fowls*
> *of the air, and to the wild beasts of the*
> *earth; that all the earth may know that*
> *there is a God in Israel."*

Often, I have wondered, "Who am I that God would know me, much less call me His own."

I have discovered that my relationship with God was His idea. He offered me the opportunity to make a life changing decision, and that was to choose to give Him my life. The decision was mine, but it was His idea to offer me such an amazing deal.

Once I made that decision my life took a drastic change. I really did not have any idea of the depth of that decision. It was as if I just signed on the dotted line without reading the particulars. I can tell you that it was the greatest decision I ever made.

In the scripture, we read of the encounter David had with the greatest enemy he had ever seen, Goliath. David had been given the word of God that he was going to be the next king of Israel. It was sometime later that he was confronted with Goliath. This whole story is powerful.

Yet, those last few words of David's statement, "That all the earth may know that there is a God in Israel," speak volumes to us when we stop and think about it.

When you or I give our lives to God, God moves inside of our lives. He tells us in Romans 8:28,

*"And, we know that all things work together
for good to them that love God, to them who
are the called according to his purpose."*

The thought that He is working in every circumstance we face should cause our faith to soar.

Every day we face situations involving people, places, or things that rise up against us. Some are so insignificant and some are as big as the giant David faced. But, I am reminded that I face these situations not because God is trying to punish me, but because He chooses to use my life to reveal to this world that there is a God inside of this child of God.

It is for this reason that I share these following situations.

God's promise to us back in 1968 was that my wife would be as a vine and my children as grapes. The power of His promise does not fade with the years. It stands like the bridge you cross every day year after year.

Jodie's baby girl, Abigail was two years old. The older kids were in their rooms as Abigail roamed the house looking for Daddy. Her Dad served as the minister of music for the church across the yard.

Abigail went to the door of the church and began to knock and call her daddy. There was no answer. She began her trip back home, only she went the wrong way. She was standing in the middle of major highway as a large truck was coming around the curve and down the hill in the lane she was in.

A car came to a screeching halt. The door opened. An arm reached out, grabbed the child and sped off. The lady then took the child to a motel nearby and asked if anyone knew this child.

The clerk said she recognized the baby and gave directions to the child's home. God prevented what could have been a terrible disaster to let us know there was a God in this family and in this child's life.

One Saturday evening my son, Jonathan and his family were on their way home from shopping. Suddenly a bullet came through the side window of the van and went out the back window. It missed the three children sitting in their car seats. This was to show once again that there was a God in the lives of these parents and these children.

Jonathan's kids were in the back of the van and their Mom was speeding down the freeway. For some reason, the van ran into the back of a dump truck. She hit the brakes. The truck sped off.

Then she pressed the accelerator and the van hit the truck again. The van looked a mess, but everyone was safe. There is a God in the lives of this family.

It was while dealing with the pain in my back that I began to think about the truth that Christ is coming back for a church without spot or wrinkle. Personally, I don't know of one. Neither do I know a person that is temple perfect.

GRANDPA, SAVE US

On a hot July day, the local radio station reported it was over 100 degrees and they were encouraging everyone to stay out of the heat as much as possible. My daughter-in-law had brought the children up to visit us. They had stopped by and picked up Abigail, Jodie's youngest daughter.

All my grandchildren love their cousins. The kids were outside under the large shade tree playing house with the tea sets and the pots and pans. Enis and I were sitting in the dining room with Rachael.

These two little boys love their Grandpa. Many times, they would wake me up asking for my "gasses" so they could preach. I would wake up and see they each had been in my closet and put on my suit including my socks and shoes. They were going to preach like Grandpa.

The girls had come into the house sat on the couch and were watching a video.

I heard an auto horn, got up and walked into the living room where the girls were and looked out the window. No one was in the yard. I looked at the TV as I was passing and thought the sound came from the movie. I returned to the conversation in the dining room.

A little while later I heard the horn blow again. I surmised the driver was blowing his horn to say good-bye on the video.

As I started to the living room again, the thought came to me, "Where are those boys?" I walked out on the front porch.

Little Jesse with his sweaty hands on the window of my van called out, "Grandpa, save us!" They had gotten into the van and couldn't get the doors open to get out. Noah had given up on getting out of the van and was about to go to sleep.

I ran and opened the door and got the boys up in my arms and took them into the house.

As I took those boys into the house I wanted to get on my face in the dirt and truly thank God for saving their lives.

Satan was trying again to rob, kill and destroy, but so the world would know that was a God in this family He rescued those little boys.

Early the next morning I was sitting in my office while the kids were still asleep.

Suddenly the door flew open and Noah with his arms opened wide announced, "I'm not dead!" I lost it again. That was wonderful news to me that day and every day.

I BELIEVE IN ANGELS

One day I was cutting my grass with my tractor and bush hog. As I was coming around a small hill, the bush hog hit an obstruction and tilted the tractor over.

I was thrown to the ground and the tractor motor and blades were still turning over on top of me. As if in slow motion, I watched the tractor roll over on top of me.

I felt the Lord say, "Just put your feet on the transmission and keep pushing as the tractor comes down on top of you."

I did as I was told. The tractor rolled over me and then on over to its side. I got up and went to see if my neighbor would come and help me turn the tractor upright so I could finish cutting my grass.

I tell you this because I also want you to know that there is a God in my life.

So, when you face your giant, realize that you are not alone. There is a God in your life.

Even if you have never accepted Him, He has never forsaken you and He is waiting for you to call on Him.

THE TORNADO

Shanna and her husband, Brian lived in the small college community, Franklin Springs, Georgia where he served as the mayor. Jodie and Dewayne were temporarily living with them in their new home. The weather looked bad that day with dark clouds hovering just above the busy activity of the day.

The phone rang just as the sirens began to blast the news of impending danger. Jodie answered the phone and Shanna said for them to get into the basement because a tornado was coming.

She and the kids got in the corner just as the power went out. The loud roar caused their ears to pop. The walls inside the basement began to move back and forth.

In a short time, they heard nothing but silence.

They walked up the steps into the hall way and then into the living room. The Baby Grand piano had been lifted and then dropped. Half of the roof had blown off the house. For some reasons, the large windows were still intact.

Outside in the cul-de-sac the high-top van was missing. The storm had picked it up and thrown it toward the house.

The front of the van hit the dirt at the edge of the paved walk way and then blew around the house.

It was as if an angel had directed its path to go around the house instead of through the large windows of the house.

Shanna and Brian's son, Evan was going to school at Athens Christian school in Athens, Georgia. The bus was scheduled to be there at the exact time the tornado hit.

However just as the bus was leaving the school, a student was acting up. The bus driver turned around and took the student back to the school. This delayed their arrival by fifteen minutes. Otherwise there could have been a school bus full of students hurt in this storm as it destroyed the city hall building along with the fire station.

People were out observing the damage in the aftermath, but there was no doubt that God had protected the citizens of this community.

For me, there was no doubt that God had protected my family. I remembered the promise, "Your wife shall be as a vine and your children as grapes." As I worshipped the Lord with the song, "Great is Thy Faithfulness."

Is this the end of my story?

I don't think so.

I just know that in all this I have seen the faithfulness of God. It is true that all things work together for our good.

While all things are not good, it's those times when the bad things are brought before our loving Heavenly Father and He turns the bad into the good.

THE DUMP TRUCK

Some years ago, I had a job driving a dump truck. For a week, I rode with another driver showing me places we got the gravel or asphalt we would be hauling. It was my first day alone.

I climbed into the old truck and began my day. We were paving a road in the mountains above Helen, Georgia. My trainer had backed his truck into the spreader to dump his load. I pulled up just above the road we were paving. I sat there waiting for him to finish and pull out. Then I would back into the spreader and dump the asphalt on my truck.

As I sat there a heard a "click," then another "click," and then "pop." The brakes had just gone out and this truck began to roll backwards down that curvy road gaining speed with every turn of the wheels.

The foreman had told me to back the truck toward the asphalt spreader. I called out to him what was happening.

He began to shout to others that we had a runaway truck. Equipment, cars, trucks, and people were in the road behind me. Steering by and looking into my mirrors, I managed to miss them all.

As I turned left and then right I was at the bottom of the incline. There was a deep drop off where the little creek ran under the road. The truck started off on my left.

I prayed, "Lord, You're up."

He said, "Just stay out of the window and you will be alright."

With a loud crash, the truck turned over on its side and landed in the creek. People were running to the scene.

I heard them say, "Is he alive? Is he ok?"

I began gathering my Bible and personal items and then began crawling out of the window above me. They put me in a pick-up truck and we rushed to the hospital.

They took x-rays and checked me over. The doctor said my vertebrae had been crushed. It wasn't long before my children were gathered at my side.

I came home and was put to bed. Jodie came and sang a song to me. I called her back two or three times to sing it again as it spoke to my heart and wounded spirit. I was hurting and did not know if I would be able to walk again or not.

She said the next time I called her to sing it again for me, "Daddy, I'm just going to give you the tape."

"For all that You've done, I will thank You.
For all that You're going to do.
For all that You've promised and all that You are
For all that has carried me through,
Jesus, I thank You.

And I thank You, thank You, Lord
And I thank You, thank You, Lord

Thank You for loving and setting me free
Thank You for giving Your life just for me
Jesus, I thank You, graciously thank You
And I thank You, thank You, Lord"

Thinking about my broken body, I began to see this picture in my mind. I hope you can see it also. One night, my wife called me to come to bed, but I wrote this poem as fast as it came to me. It's called "The Great Shepherd."

THE GREAT SHEPHERD

The streets were crowded when He came into town
Folks just stopped and looked around
As He made His way down the street
They just stared at this stranger's
Maimed and wounded sheep

With everyone's desire to have perfect Temple sheep
They had brought from miles around
The best that could be found
Those worthy of their keep.

Why, who is this that would dare
To show in this Holy place,
Such a flock of wounded and maimed sheep?
Why, it's just a disgrace!

He spoke not a word,
But led us to the fold
Though He was tired, weary and cold.

The great day came when the sheep were to be presented
Each Ewe and each lamb marched down the aisle
As they played softly, "Just As I Am."

We listened closely as their stats were read
For they were meticulously groomed,
And very well fed.
The judge would nod and the crowd would cheer.

Then it was time for the Stranger's sheep to appear.
A hush fell over the crowd. It grew deathly quiet.
Then Ol' Sam, the first sheep came into sight.

The crowd roared with laughter
And some began to sneer as other swore and said,
"What are they doing here?"

Briskly the judge's hand was raised
The noise died down as each man regained his place.
The judge leaned over the rail,
And looked into the face of a sheep with one eye,
"Tell us what you have to say."

"Sir, we were on the hillside and all was quiet
When a huge bear gave a terrible roar
It was a fright.
His wide swing was meant for my head to be displaced

When my Shepherd jumped on its back
And I was saved by His grace.
What was meant for the end of me
Cost only one eye,
But, hey, I can still see.

"And you, sir," the judge went on,
"Tell us how it is that
One of your ears is gone!"

The sheep moved closer
To its shepherd to stand
And felt the loving touch
Of a strong right hand.

"The lion was still in the tall grass
Just lying in wait for me to pass.
When with a roar, up he came and in a flash,
My shepherd had hold of its mane.
Its jaws snapped as I stood frozen with fear,

But when it was all over,
Huh, I'm missing only an ear.
So, here I stand on this Holy ground,
For Sir, I came just as I am."

"He's our shepherd", another sheep chimed,
"For He rescued each of us, and just in time.
Oh, we are not our own,
We were bought with a price,
He thought each of us worthy enough
That He was willing to die."

"Oh, what a shepherd!"
The crowd began to say
For all their imperfections
Were covered by His grace.

One by one they came,
The scarred, the bruised and the maimed.
Each of their stories was just about the same.
But one thing you could compare,
When they were in need, He was always there.

Oh, He is the great shepherd,
Not just some "Little Bo-Peep."
I ought to know, for I am one of His sheep.
We were all in, as the new day had begun
I heard them say, "Thank You, Father."
"Oh, You're welcome, Son."

AN ODE TO THE ANT

You are to be studied up close
By folks from afar
Who are to consider your characteristics
What a wonder from God you are

You are a creature so tiny
Yet, one so strong
Your load is more than your weight
You work hard and long.

You find your place in the colony
Worker, queen, or drone,
You live to serve others
For your life is not just your own

Life's substance is where you find it
You work to bring it in store
After the long hard struggle
You turn and go back for more.

There is no set time for you to work
Whether it is day or night
As long as there is work to do

You keep at it with all your might.
But we get tired
And often complain
About life's futility
And our aches and pains

Just how do you do it, little one?
It's plain to see,
Lord, whatever you put in that little ant,
Would You please put some in me?

"Yes, but I'll have to change your nature,"
I seem to hear Him chide,
"for it's not what's on your calendar,
But what you have inside."

So, if in this life
I ever become a saint,
It will be because I considered
"An Ode To The Ant."

THE DAY THE TREE CAME DOWN

It was in the old church yard
When in silence that day
A new life began
In just this way

From the old tree
The little acorn fell.
What would be its future?
No one could tell.
But in God's mind
He had a plan,
For something great
Over time's span

A gentle breeze
Began to blow
Till the little acorn
Did not show
The dust and dirt
 Began to gather
Just to protect it
From the weather

It was in this darkness
That new life was seen
Soon it raised its head
And looked out at the green
Now it stands,
Slender and tall
Perhaps it will be a tree,
After all

Its tender limbs
Were often broken on Sundays
And used for a switch
To change a young child's
Erring ways
As the years go by,
Ring upon ring
The squirrels and birds
Have come
To do their thing

The little tree
Has faithfully
Stood and watched over its post
Not as an enemy to any,
But as a friend to most
The kids would climb the tree
And sit on the limb
From here they could see forever,
According to them.

In its shade
There were dinners
A few times a year.
It was always there
To shade the horses…
Until they disappeared.
First there was the Model T
Then the Model A
Then it was the modern cars
That enjoyed the shade

From opened windows
Music filled the air
With songs of glorious praise
That the people would sing.
Now the windows are closed
Because of air conditioning
The singing has changed
And the crowds have too
But the old oak tree has been faithful
All the years through.

The old tree watched
As on the hillside,
A little to the west
Families gather
To lay their loved ones to rest

Now, here lies the old man,
But how can it be?
Not long ago
He was the child,
Climbing this tree.

But now we have built
A new building
As we plan
To reach the youth.
And, old tree
You are in the way
And of no further use.

If this old tree could talk
It could tell you a thing or two
About the relationship it had
With all of the former youth.

Now where the old tree once stood
There is a neat little stack of wood.
It's all over as anyone can tell,
Except… perhaps…
From the old oak tree
A little acorn fell.

THE END

I DON'T THINK SO!